Dedication

To Our Lady
of the Holy Name of God

&

To all who kneel
at the foot of the Cross and
before the Blessed Sacrament
seeking mercy, healing,
and the love that saves.

May the Lord bless you and keep you.
May the Lord let His Face shine upon you
and be gracious to you.
May the Lord look upon you kindly
and bring you peace.

Published by: Bishop Sheen Today

www.bishopsheentoday.com

Title: The Sheen Mission Series Collected Meditations: A Fourfold Mission of Reparation and Love on the Holy Face, the Blessed Virgin Mary, the Cross, the Eucharist and the Mission of Christ

Compiled by Allan J. Smith. Includes bibliographical references.
Identifiers: Paperback: 978-1-997931-00-3
eBook: 978-1-997627-88-3
Hardcover: 978-1-997931-07-2

Subjects: Holy Face of Jesus – St. Thérèse of Lisieux – Blessed Virgin Mary – The Cross – the Seven Last Words – The Eucharist — Prayer and Meditation – Archbishop Fulton J. Sheen – Lives of the Saints

THE SHEEN MISSION SERIES COLLECTED MEDITATIONS

A Fourfold Mission
of Reparation and Love
on the Holy Face,
the Blessed Virgin Mary,
the Cross, the Eucharist
and the Mission of Christ

Allan Smith

FOREWORD
to the Collected Edition

The Sheen Mission Series:
A Fourfold Journey of Reparation and Love

In every age, the Church is renewed when souls return to the essentials: to Christ crucified, to His Eucharistic Face, to the Mother He gave us, and to the mission He entrusts to His people. This *Collected Edition* gathers together four pilgrim paths that were first published as individual booklets. Each was written to guide the faithful into deeper intimacy with Our Lord, drawing upon the wisdom of Archbishop Fulton J. Sheen and the Little Way of St. Thérèse of Lisieux.

These four volumes form a single spiritual arc:

- **The Holy Face and the Little Way** introduces us to the hidden Face of Christ, bruised yet radiant, and calls us to the work of reparation through small, hidden acts of love.

- **Behold Your Mother** draws us beneath the Cross with Mary, the Sorrowful Mother, to learn compassion, perseverance, and the power of her maternal intercession.

- **The Cross and the Last Words** brings us to Calvary itself, where Sheen's preaching on the Seven Last Words reveals Christ's supreme lesson in love, mercy, and surrender.

- **Lord, Show Us Thy Face and We Shall Be Saved** sends us forth on mission, reminding us that contemplation leads to transformation, and that the world must see the Face of Christ shining through our lives.

Taken together, these meditations are not merely theological reflections; they are a retreat in print. They invite us to sit in silence before the Eucharist, to console the pierced Hearts of Jesus and Mary, and to join Sheen in the lifelong practice of the daily Holy Hour.

Archbishop Sheen often said, "The greatest love story of all time is contained in a tiny white Host." Each page of this collection seeks to draw you closer to that Love. It is a summons to prayer, a call to reparation, and an invitation to mission.

May these meditations awaken in you the longing of the Psalmist: *"Let Your Face shine upon us, Lord, and we shall be saved"* (Psalm 80:3). May they lead you to gaze upon His countenance more often, to imitate His Mother more faithfully, to carry His Cross more courageously, and to radiate His light more clearly in the world.

And above all, may you discover in this journey what Sheen himself discovered: *that the only tragedy is not to be a saint.*

How to Use This Book

This Collected Edition of the **Sheen Mission Series** is meant to be more than a book — it is a retreat in print. Each page is an invitation to prayer, reparation, and deeper union with Christ through the wisdom of Archbishop Fulton J. Sheen and the witness of St. Thérèse of Lisieux.

A Retreat in Print

The five parts of this book follow a spiritual arc:

- **The Holy Face and the Little Way** – encountering Christ in hiddenness and love.

- **Behold Your Mother** – standing with Mary at the Cross.

- **The Cross and the Last Words** – meditating on Calvary with Sheen.

- **Lord, Show Us Thy Face and We Shall Be Saved** – living the Eucharistic mission of Christ in the world.

- **Overcoming Sin, Practicing Virtue, and Living the Beatitudes** – A mission of interior renewal and divine transformation.

You may read these parts in sequence as a sustained journey, or pause and dwell with one theme at a time.

For Daily Prayer

Archbishop Sheen often urged the faithful to make a **daily Holy Hour** before the Blessed Sacrament. This book is designed to support that practice. You might:

- Read one chapter slowly during your Holy Hour.

- Linger over the Scripture passages and allow silence to follow.

- Conclude with one of the prayers from this book.

Even if you cannot make a full Holy Hour, these meditations can be prayed in shorter moments throughout the day.

For Retreats

This collection lends itself well to parish missions, small-group retreats, or personal days of recollection. Each part can be used as a **retreat theme** — whether for one day, a triduum, or a full week of prayer.

A Word of Encouragement

Read slowly. Pray deeply. Let these pages lead you from contemplation to imitation, from silence before the Holy Face to mission in the world. As Archbishop Sheen taught, *"The greatest love story of all time is contained in a tiny white Host."* May this book help you to discover, day by day, that love story anew.

Table of Contents

PART II
BEHOLD YOUR MOTHER

PART III
THE CROSS AND THE LAST WORDS

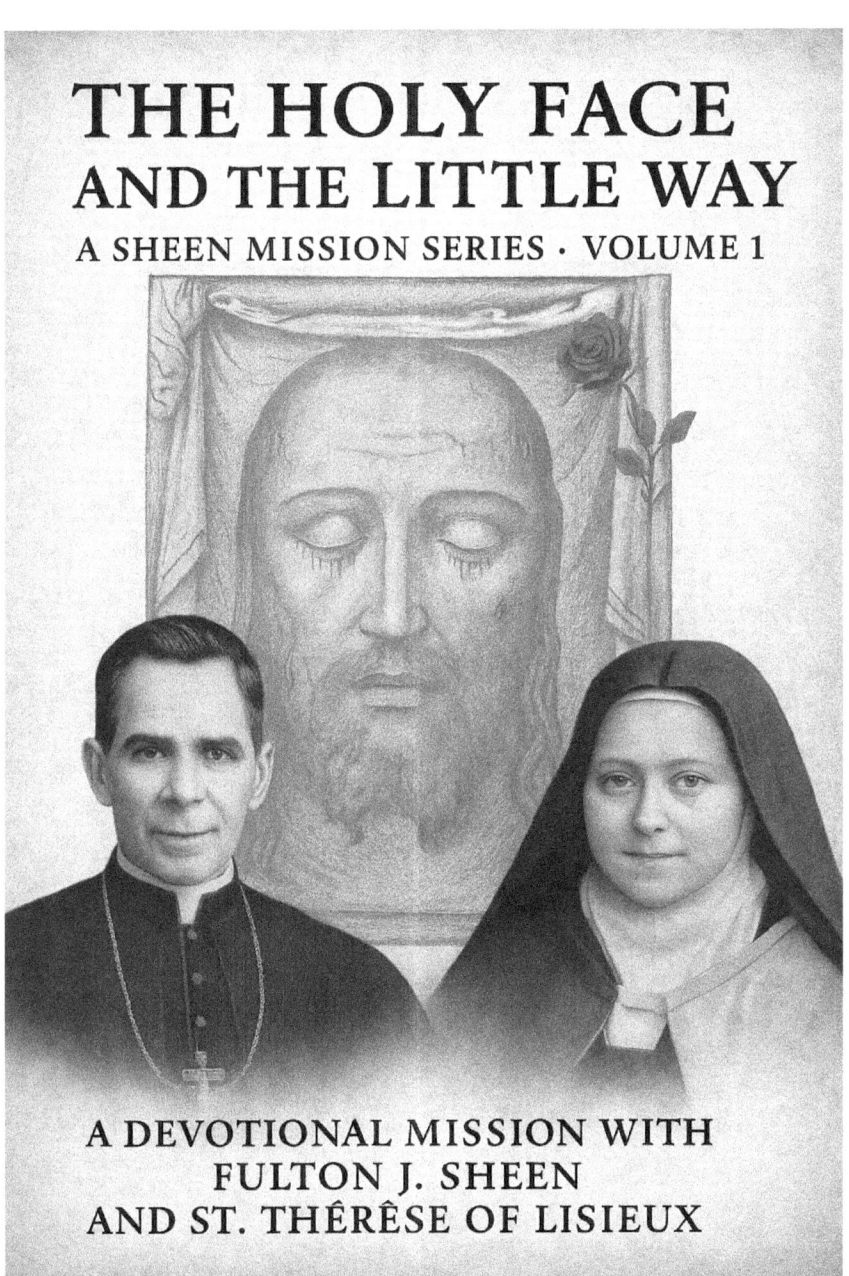

THE HOLY FACE
AND THE LITTLE WAY
A SHEEN MISSION SERIES · VOLUME 1

A DEVOTIONAL MISSION WITH
FULTON J. SHEEN
AND ST. THÉRÊSE OF LISIEUX

THE HOLY FACE AND THE LITTLE WAY

A Devotional Mission with Fulton J. Sheen
and St. Thérèse of Lisieux.
A Sheen Mission Series - Volume I

The Sheen Mission Series invites you to walk with Archbishop Fulton J. Sheen in prayer, reparation, and renewal — a journey of the Holy Face, the Cross, the Eucharist and Our Blessed Mother.

Description:

The Holy Face and the Little Way is the first volume in the Sheen Mission Series — a prayerful journey inspired by the spirituality of Archbishop Fulton J. Sheen and St. Thérèse of Lisieux.

In these pages, you will discover how the "Little Way" of trust and love is united to the devotion of the Holy Face of Jesus. This treasury includes meditations, prayers, and reflections that will guide you into deeper union with Christ through adoration, reparation, and confidence in His merciful love.

> *"One of the greatest tragedies in the world is wasted pain. Pain without relation to the Cross is like an unsigned check — without value. But once we have it countersigned with the Signature of the Saviour on the Cross, it takes on an infinite value."*

— Archbishop Fulton J. Sheen

2

FOREWORD

There is a Face behind the silence of the Eucharist. A Face behind the veil of suffering. A Face behind the hiddenness of love. This book is an invitation to gaze upon that Face — the bruised, radiant, sorrowful, and saving Face of Christ.

Archbishop Fulton J. Sheen once said, 'The world's greatest need is to rediscover the true image of Christ's Face — a Face of mercy, not judgment; of tenderness, not wrath.' He believed that before we reform the world, we must first adore. And before we preach, we must first look — silently, lovingly — upon the Holy Face of Jesus.

In these pages, you will find a sacred meeting between the wisdom of Sheen and the heart of St. Thérèse of Lisieux. Two souls who, though separated by time and vocation, both found their mission in loving the Face of the Crucified One. St. Thérèse once wrote, 'Thy Face is my only wealth... I no longer ask for anything but love.' Fulton Sheen would echo her sentiment in his own way: 'It is not what we do for Christ that makes us holy — it is what we allow Him to do in us.

This book is not a theological treatise or a spiritual manual. It is a pilgrimage. A series of reflections, devotions, and meditations meant to draw you closer to the One who hides Himself in silence, and who reveals Himself in love.

May every page lead you to the Face of Christ. And may that Face — once looked upon — never be forgotten.

INTRODUCTION

Why the Holy Face? Why Now?

We live in an age of distractions. Noise fills our minds, screens occupy our attention, and our hearts often wander, numb from the weight of the world's demands. In the midst of this, the Holy Face of Christ calls us — quietly, insistently — to return. To remember. To behold.

Why the Holy Face? Because it is the most human part of Christ, and the most wounded. It is the part we spit upon in sin and the part we seek in sorrow. The Face reveals the Person. And the bruised Face of Jesus reveals the cost of love, the depth of mercy, and the grief of forgotten intimacy.

Why now? Because the world has forgotten how to blush. Archbishop Sheen wrote, 'The greatest loss of our time is the loss of the sense of sin.' And what restores it? A Face that suffers silently. A Face that absorbs hatred without retaliation. A Face that still looks upon us with love.

This devotion is not sentimental. It is not sweet. It is soul-rending. It asks us to look upon what we have done to Love — and to make reparation not out of guilt, but out of desire. Desire to console. Desire to remain. Desire to love more purely in a world that loves too little.

In these chapters, you will walk with Fulton Sheen and St. Thérèse. You will be invited to kneel, to look, and to let the Holy Face imprint itself upon your soul. And if you let it, you will never look at the Cross — or at another soul — the same way again.

Why the Holy Face? Why now? Because Christ is still asking, 'Who will stay with Me?' And the only worthy answer is the offering of your heart.

MEDITATION 1

The Hidden Face of God
and the Mission of Love

Archbishop Fulton Sheen often said that the greatest tragedy of modern times is not rebellion, but forgetfulness. We have not so much rejected God — we have simply ignored His Face.

He warned that when man loses the sense of sin, he loses the capacity to recognize the sacred. The Eucharist becomes a symbol. The Cross, a decoration. And the Face of Christ? Hidden behind the veil of indifference.

But St. Thérèse saw that Face. She called it "the only beauty that ravished my heart." And rather than run from it, she leaned in. She saw His bruises as invitations. His silence is speech. And she made of her life one long act of reparation.

Fulton Sheen was drawn to the mystery of reparation — that the greatest love we can show to God is not in words, but in willingly standing beside Him in silence, when others flee. This is what the saints did. This is what St. Thérèse did. This is what we are invited to do.

To contemplate the Holy Face of Christ is not just a private devotion. It is a mission. It is to become a Veronica in a world that spits and turns away — to wipe the Face of Christ by acts of love, adoration, sacrifice, and fidelity.

In this age of noise, distraction, and spiritual amnesia, we are called to remember the Face that loved us unto death. The bruised Face. The silent Face. The Holy Face.

This book is a pilgrimage with two great souls — Fulton Sheen and St. Thérèse — who beckon us toward that Face, not only to gaze upon it, but to carry its imprint into the world.

Let us begin — not with many words, but with hearts open to the Face of Love, hidden and holy.

MEDITATION 2

St. Thérèse and the Offering of the Face

In the cloistered silence of Lisieux, a young Carmelite nun once knelt before a simple image: the Holy Face of Jesus. It was not majestic. It was not beautiful by worldly standards. It was bruised, spat upon, and crowned with thorns.

Yet St. Thérèse of the Child Jesus saw in that disfigured face the deepest truth of God's love — a love that hides itself, suffers silently, and offers itself without complaint.

Long before she would consecrate herself to Merciful Love, St. Thérèse gave herself to the Face of Christ. She joined the Archconfraternity of the Holy Face and even added the title 'of the Holy Face' to her religious name. This was not pious decoration — it was identity. It was a mission. It was her way of standing beside the Suffering Servant when so many turned away.

For St. Thérèse, the Holy Face was not a separate devotion; it was the very heart of her Little Way. She believed that to console Jesus in His hidden sufferings was the greatest act of love. And she did it not with grand acts or public witness, but with the offering of small things — accepted in silence, embraced in love, given without seeking praise.

Each annoyance, each trial, each moment of dryness in prayer became for her a veil lifted — an opportunity to see and kiss the wounds of Christ. She would say, 'I want to love Jesus so much, to console Him so much, that He will be forced to do my will — by doing His!'

And what was His will? That she should love Him in littleness, serve Him in obscurity, and console Him in His agony — not with words, but with trust.

To walk with St. Thérèse is to discover that the bruised Face of Christ is not a place of fear, but of encounter. It is where saints are born, and where sinners find mercy. It is where the mission of love begins.

MEDITATION 3

Reparation and the Radiance of the Hidden Christ

Reparation. It is a word that sounds severe to modern ears. Yet it is the language of love — not the love of sentiment, but of sacrifice. To make reparation is to offer something back to God, not because He needs it, but because we have wounded what is most beautiful: His love.

Fulton Sheen once said that we do not hate God; we simply forget Him. That is the great crime of the modern age — not defiance, but indifference. The Face of Christ is no longer rejected with fists, but ignored with shrugs. And so the Church, like Veronica, is called not to argue but to console.

Reparation begins in the heart. It is the silent 'I'm sorry' whispered before the Blessed Sacrament. It is the soul who kneels in a dark chapel while the world spins on in noise. It is the mother who offers her sleepless night, the priest who offers his hidden suffering, the child who accepts a small humiliation with love.

St. Thérèse understood that reparation was not about grand gestures, but about the quiet giving of self in union with Christ. She did not seek to escape suffering, but to infuse it with purpose. Every cough, every dryness in prayer, every misunderstanding — she kissed them like the bruises on His Face.

Fulton Sheen echoed this when he wrote, 'The greatest love is not to proclaim Christ but to suffer with Him.' In this way, reparation becomes radiant. It is not bitter; it is beautiful. It does not draw attention to itself, but to Him. It restores what sin disfigures — not with vengeance, but with love.

In contemplating the Holy Face, we are drawn into this divine exchange. We see not just what sin has done to God, but what love has done for us. We gaze upon His wounds and discover our mission: to return love for love, silence for mockery, fidelity for betrayal.

This is reparation: the radiant response of a soul who sees the Face of Christ and refuses to turn away.

MEDITATION 4

The Holy Hour and
the Veronica Vocation

In the Stations of the Cross, there is one encounter that stands out not for its drama, but for its intimacy: Veronica steps forward, breaks through the crowd, and wipes the Face of Jesus. She says nothing. She makes no speech. But her veil absorbs the blood and sweat of the Saviour, and her act becomes a Gospel of its own.

Archbishop Fulton Sheen often reflected on this moment. To him, Veronica represented every soul who dares to console Christ in a world that crucifies Him daily. Her gesture was reparation — not with sermons, but with tenderness, not with power, but with presence.

The Holy Hour, as Sheen practiced and preached it, is our way of becoming Veronica. When we kneel before the Eucharistic Christ, we are not merely fulfilling a devotion — we are wiping His Face. We are telling Him, with our silence and stillness, that He is not forgotten.

Fulton Sheen called the Holy Hour a 'daily hour of companionship with Christ.' He urged priests and laypeople alike to spend sixty minutes each day with the Eucharistic Lord. Not for results, not for mystical experiences, but for love. For fidelity. For reparation.

St. Thérèse lived her Holy Hours in the hidden cloister of Lisieux. She had no chapel of exposition, no public platform. But she made of her duties, her prayers, and her little sacrifices a perpetual Holy Hour of the heart. She was a Veronica in silence, in sickness, in surrender.

To be a Veronica today is to go against the grain. It is to pause when others rush, to adore when others ignore, to enter the chapel when the world beckons us to scroll and scatter. But it is also to discover a beauty beyond words — the beauty of the Face of Christ etched upon our soul.

Let us enter the Holy Hour not as spectators, but as lovers. Let us become Veronicas. And let us never leave the Face of Christ untouched by our love.

MEDITATION 5

The Little Way of Reparation

St. Thérèse once wrote, 'I have always wanted to be a saint... but I have always felt that I was incapable of great deeds.' It was this very awareness — her littleness — that led her to discover the path now known around the world as the Little Way.

The Little Way is not about doing less. It is about doing with greater love. It is about doing the unnoticed, the uncelebrated, the mundane — with the heart of one who knows Christ is watching.

For St. Thérèse, the Little Way became a school of reparation. She embraced daily annoyances, hidden sufferings, and acts of obedience as offerings to the Holy Face. Each small surrender became a kiss upon the bruises of Christ's love.

She understood that she could not ascend the mountain of perfection by her own strength. Instead, she would let Jesus lift her, like a child reaching upward with empty hands. Her smallness became her strength. Her weakness, her offering.

Archbishop Fulton Sheen echoed this when he wrote that sanctity is not about doing great things for God, but doing small things with great fidelity to His will. Reparation, he taught, begins with the acceptance of the present moment — without complaint, without spectacle, without applause.

In a world obsessed with results, St. Thérèse teaches us that love does not measure itself by success. It measures itself by surrender. It is not how much we do, but how much we yield — how much we allow ourselves to be poured out in silence, for love alone.

The Little Way is not an escape from the cross; it is a hidden path into its heart. It is there, on the narrow road of daily sacrifice, that the Holy Face shines — not in majesty, but in mercy.

Let us walk this way. Let us make our lives a mosaic of hidden offerings. Let us become saints — not by great deeds, but by great love.

MEDITATION 6

The Consoling Gaze

There is a kind of healing that happens not through words, but through gaze. A glance that understands. A look that listens. In the spiritual life, it is not always what we say to God that matters most — it is how we allow ourselves to be seen by Him.

St. Thérèse often wrote about looking upon the Face of Jesus. For her, it was not an image to admire, but a place to rest. A sanctuary for her soul. She did not need to explain herself in prayer. She simply placed herself before Him — silent, still, and seen.

Fulton Sheen understood this, too. His Holy Hours were less about speaking and more about gazing — fixing his eyes on the Eucharist until the gaze of Christ began to change him. He called it 'radiation therapy for the soul.' We become what we behold.

In a world that stares but does not see, the Holy Face calls us back to the power of presence. In Adoration, we come not to perform, but to console. We let the eyes of Christ meet our wounds. We let His silence absorb our noise. We allow His gaze to say what words cannot.

Reparation is born in this gaze. When we behold the disfigured Face of Christ and still find beauty, we begin to see as God sees. We begin to recognize the value of souls, the dignity of suffering, and the hiddenness of grace.

St. Thérèse believed that just one glance of love toward the Face of Christ could change a heart, lift a soul, and bring consolation to a God so often forgotten. She gave Him her gaze — not once, but daily. In doing so, she received His peace.

Let us return our gaze to Christ. Let us adore Him with the eyes of the heart. And let us never forget that in every Holy Hour, He gazes back.

MEDITATION 7

The Interior Life and
the Hidden Christ

The world today is noisy. Its rhythms are rushed, its values external, and its heroes often loud. But the saints teach us that holiness grows in silence. Intimacy with God is not born in the glare of applause, but in the quiet of the interior life.

St. Thérèse lived almost her entire vocation in obscurity. Her greatness was not seen, not praised, not published — until after her death. She was hidden, like the Eucharist. And it was there, in that hiddenness, that her intimacy with Christ deepened beyond words.

Fulton Sheen emphasized again and again that the strength of a priest, of a layperson, of the Church itself, depends on the interior life. He wrote, 'The future of the world and of the Church passes through the family and through the interior life of its members.' This interior life — rooted in prayer, silence, and self-gift — is the soil of sanctity.

The Holy Face devotion is a direct invitation into the interior life. We are not asked to do something dramatic, but to look deeply, silently, reverently. To behold the Face of Christ is to begin a conversation of the soul, a love that grows wordlessly in the heart's sanctuary.

Reparation begins here. Not in public penance, but in hidden offerings. Not in declarations, but in desires. The desire to love, to repair, to remain — even when unseen, even when un-thanked. Especially then.

St. Thérèse knew that interior silence was the womb of divine action. She said, 'My vocation is love.' And love, she knew, is most fruitful when it is most free of self.

Let us cultivate this interior garden — not with striving, but with surrender. Let us meet the hidden Christ with hidden hearts. And there, in the silence, let the Holy Face become the mirror in which we are formed anew.

MEDITATION 8

The Cross and the Countenance of Mercy

The Holy Face of Jesus is inseparable from the Cross. It is there, on Calvary, that the Face is most revealed — bruised, broken, and yet radiant with mercy.

St. Thérèse wrote, 'It is through suffering that I have come to love the Cross.' She understood that the Cross was not a contradiction of God's love, but its most eloquent expression. To love the Face of Christ is to accept the shadow of the Cross, not as punishment, but as participation.

Fulton Sheen, too, placed the Cross at the center of the spiritual life. He saw in the Passion not only the redemption of man, but the unveiling of the divine heart. He said, 'Unless there is a Good Friday in your life, there can be no Easter Sunday.

The Countenance of Christ crucified is not a face of defeat. It is the Face of mercy, poured out. Every wound becomes a word, every drop of blood a prayer, every silence an act of surrender.

To contemplate the Holy Face is to enter into the Paschal Mystery — to unite our sufferings with His, to offer our lives in reparation, and to be transformed by love that does not flee from the Cross.

St. Thérèse did not seek suffering, but she did not run from it. She saw it as her way to love more, to console Jesus more, to become more like Him. And through that suffering, she radiated joy — not superficial cheer, but the deep peace of a soul resting in the will of God.

We, too, are called to let the Cross etch itself onto our hearts. Not as a burden alone, but as a blessing. Not as death, but as a door.

Let us lift our gaze to the Holy Face on the Cross. Let it teach us what love looks like when it is poured out. And let our lives become a reflection of that Countenance — a mirror of mercy in a world in need of hope.

MEDITATION 9

Love Alone Remains

There comes a point on the spiritual path when everything else falls away — the consolations, the clarity, even the strength we once felt. What remains is love. Love, not as a feeling, but as a decision. Love, not as fireworks, but as faithfulness.

St. Thérèse knew this well. Her final months were marked by darkness, dryness, and even doubt. Yet she chose to love. She smiled through her sufferings. She prayed when she felt nothing. She offered everything to Jesus with empty hands, saying, 'I choose all!'

Fulton Sheen taught that sanctity is not measured by visions or miracles, but by how much we allow Christ to live in us. He wrote, 'Christ is not loved because He is not known; and He is not known because His Face is not looked upon.' St. Thérèse looked — and she loved, even when that Face seemed hidden.

To love in darkness is the highest act of faith. To say, 'Though He slay me, yet will I trust in Him,' is to echo the words of Job and the soul of St. Thérèse. It is to become reparation not just in action, but in being.

The Holy Face calls us to this surrender. To love for the sake of love. To remain faithful when everything else fades. To become, like Veronica and St. Thérèse, a resting place for Christ in a world of rejection.

When all is stripped away, love remains. And if we choose to remain in love, we remain in Him. That is the Little Way. That is the mystery of the Holy Face. That is the path of saints.

Let us end where we began — with a glance toward the Face of Christ. Let that glance become a gaze. Let that gaze become a gift. And let our hearts, like St. Thérèse's, whisper even in silence: 'My vocation is love.'

MEDITATION 10

A Mission of Reparation

The journey does not end at the feet of Christ — it begins there. Having contemplated His Holy Face, having walked the path of silence, suffering, and surrender, we now rise to carry that Face into the world.

Reparation is not only a devotion; it is a mission. The bruises we have kissed in Adoration now appear on the faces of the forgotten. The silence we have kept with Christ is now needed in a world drowning in noise.

St. Thérèse once said, 'I would spend my heaven doing good on earth.' Her Little Way did not end in the cloister; it radiated outward. It became a light for missionaries, parents, priests, and ordinary souls who long to love heroically in hidden ways.

Fulton Sheen challenged every Christian to be an apostle of the Holy Hour, a consoler of Christ, and a mirror of His mercy. He believed reparation would renew the Church, not through programs or platforms, but through saints who kneel, adore, and offer.

You are part of this mission now. Your glance, your silence, your hidden act of love — these are not forgotten. They rise like incense before the throne of God. They wipe the Face of Christ in places where His Name is ignored, and His love refused.

To live this mission is not to do more — it is to love more. To be available to grace. To be faithful in small things. To adore, to suffer, to rejoice — with Christ, for souls, in secret.

The Holy Face is not just a devotion to admire. It is a calling to answer. It is Christ, looking at you with eyes that say, 'Will you stay with Me?'

Let your answer be the life you live. Let your yes be daily. And let your heart, like St. Thérèse and Fulton Sheen, become a living veil — a place where the Holy Face finds rest, and the world finds hope.

Quotes from St. Thérèse of Lisieux and Archbishop Fulton J. Sheen

Quotes from St. Thérèse of Lisieux

"Thy Face is my only wealth. I ask nothing more."

"Jesus, Your Face is the only homeland of my heart."

"To live of love is to dry Your Face, to console You every hour of the day."

"I want to spend my heaven doing good on earth."

"I choose all! I want everything that Jesus wills for me."

"It is confidence and nothing but confidence that must lead us to Love."

*"Suffering is the very best gift He has to give us.
He gives it only to His chosen friends."*

*"I am not afraid of the darkness. My God, may Your Face
shine on me only for a moment... and I shall be saved."*

Quotes from Archbishop Fulton J. Sheen

"Christ is not loved because He is not known;
and He is not known because His Face is not looked upon."

"Unless there is a Good Friday in your life, there can be no Easter Sunday."

"The greatest love story of all time is contained in a tiny white Host."

"The world's greatest need is to rediscover the true image of Christ's Face
— a Face of mercy, not judgment; of tenderness, not wrath."

"The modern man has everything — except self-knowledge and God-awareness."

"We become like that which we gaze upon. Looking into a sunset, the face takes
on a golden glow. Looking at the Holy Face of Christ, the soul does likewise."

"You must remember to love people and use things,
rather than to love things and use people."

"The Holy Hour becomes like an oxygen tank to revive the breath of the
Holy Spirit in the midst of the foul atmosphere of the world."

Scripture for Holy Hour Reflection

These Scripture passages have been selected to deepen one's meditation during a Holy Hour. They focus on the themes of the Holy Face, suffering, reparation, love, silence, and intimacy with God.

Psalm 27:8 – "Of you my heart has spoken: 'Seek his face.' It is your face, O Lord, that I seek."

Psalm 31:16 – "Let your face shine upon your servant; save me in your merciful love."

Psalm 80:3 – "Restore us, O God; let your face shine, that we may be saved."

Isaiah 53:2–5 – "He had no form or majesty that we should look at him, no beauty that we should desire him… He was despised and rejected by men; a man of sorrows… by his wounds we are healed."

Lamentations 3:28 – "Let him sit alone in silence when it is laid upon him."

Daniel 9:17 – "Now therefore, O our God, listen to the prayer of your servant… and cause your face to shine upon your sanctuary."

Matthew 26:38–40 – "Could you not watch one hour with me?"

Luke 22:61 – "The Lord turned and looked at Peter… and he went out and wept bitterly."

John 14:9 – "Whoever has seen me has seen the Father."

John 19:5 – "Jesus came out, wearing the crown of thorns and the purple robe. Pilate said to them, 'Behold the man!' "

2 Corinthians 4:6 – "God… has shone in our hearts to give the light of the knowledge of the glory of God in the face of Christ."

Hebrews 12:2–3 – "Looking to Jesus, the pioneer and perfecter of our faith… who endured the cross, despising the shame… Consider him who endured from sinners such hostility against himself, so that you may not grow weary or fainthearted."

Fulton Sheen's
Holy Hour Reflections

Why Make a Holy Hour

The purpose of these meditations is to aid souls in securing an inner peace by meditating for one continuous hour a day on God and our immortal destiny. Whether or not one uses these meditations does not matter in the least. Some Jews, some Protestants, and some Catholics may find it very unsatisfactory. If, however, they reject these because they wish to make the Holy Hour in their own way, they will have achieved its purpose. What is vital is not that these meditations be used, but that there be meditation.

But why spend an hour a day in meditation? Because we are living on the surface of our souls, knowing little of either God or our inner self. Our knowledge is mostly about things, not about destiny. Most of our difficulties and disappointments in life are due to mistakes in our life plans. Having forgotten the purpose of living, we have doubted even the value of living. A broken bone gives pain because it is not where it ought to be; our souls are in agony because we are not tending to the fullness of Life, Truth, and Love, which is God.

But Why Make a Holy Hour?

Here are Ten Reasons.

1. Because it is time spent in the Presence of Our Lord Himself, if faith is alive, no further reason is needed.

2. Because in our busy life, it takes considerable time to shake off the "noonday devils," the worldly cares, which cling to our souls, like dust. An hour with Our Lord follows the experience of the disciples on the road to Emmaus (Luke 24:13-35). We begin by walking with Our Lord, but our eyes are "held fast" so that we do not "recognize him". Next, He converses with our soul as we read the Scriptures. The third stage is one of sweet intimacy, as when 'he sat down at the table with them.' The fourth stage is the full dawning of the mystery of the Eucharist. Our eyes are "opened," and we recognize Him. Finally, we reach the point where we do not want to leave. The hour seemed so short. As we arise, we ask:

    Weren't our hearts burning within us when he spoke to us on the road, and when he made the Scriptures plain to us? (Luke 24:32)

3. Because Our Lord asked for it.

    Had you no strength, then, to watch with me even for an hour? (Matt. 26:40)

    The word was addressed to Peter, but he is referred to as Simon. It is our Simon-nature which needs the hour. If the hour seems hard, it is because … the spirit is willing enough, but the flesh is weak. (Mark 14:39)

4. Because the Holy Hour keeps a balance between the spiritual and the practical. Western philosophies tend to an activism in which God does nothing, and man everything; the Eastern philosophies tend to a quietism in which God does everything, and man nothing. The golden mean is in the words of St.

Thomas: "action following rest," Martha walking with Mary. The Holy Hour unites the contemplative to the active life of the person.

Thanks to the hour with Our Lord, our meditations and resolutions pass from the conscious to the subconscious and then become motives of action. A new spirit begins to pervade our work. The change is effected by Our Lord, Who fills our heart and works through our hands. A person can give only what he possesses. To give Christ to others, one must possess Him.

5.   Because the Holy Hour will make us practice what we preach.

Here is an image, he said, of the kingdom of heaven; there was once a king, who held a marriage feast for his son, and sent out his servants with a summons to all those whom he had invited to the wedding; but they would not come. (Matt. 22:2, 3)

It was written of Our Lord that He 'set out to do and to teach' (Acts 1:1). The person who practices the Holy Hour will find that when he teaches, the people will say of him as of the Lord:

All ... were astonished at the gracious words which came from his mouth. (Luke 4:22)

6.   Because the Holy Hour helps us make reparation both for the sins of the world and for our own. When the Sacred Heart appeared to St. Margaret Mary, it was His Heart, and not His Head, that was crowned with thorns. It was Love that was hurt. Black Masses, sacrilegious communions, scandals, militant atheism – who will make up for them? Who will be an Abraham for Sodom, a Mary for those who have no wine? The sins of the world are our sins as if we had committed them. If they caused Our Lord a bloody sweat, to the point that He upbraided His disciples for failing to stay with Him an hour, shall we with Cain ask:

Is it for me to watch over my brother?   (Gen. 4:9)

32

7. Because it reduces our liability to temptation and weakness. Presenting ourselves before Our Lord in the Blessed Sacrament is like putting a tubercular patient in good air and sunlight. The virus of our sins cannot long exist in the face of the Light of the world.

    Always I can keep the Lord within sight; always he is at my right hand, to make me stand firm. (Psalm 15:8)

    Our sinful impulses are prevented from arising through the barrier erected each day by the Holy Hour. Our will becomes disposed to goodness with little conscious effort on our part. Satan, the roaring lion, was not permitted to put forth his hand to touch righteous Job until he received permission (Job 1:12). Certainly then will the Lord withhold serious fall from him who watches (1 Cor. 10:13). With full confidence in his Eucharistic Lord, the person will have a spiritual resiliency. He will bounce back quickly after a falling: Fall I, it is but to rise again, sit I in darkness, the Lord will be my light. The Lord's displeasure I must bear, I that have sinned against him, till at last, he admits my plea, and grants redress. (Micah 7:8, 9)

    The Lord will be favourable even to the weakest of us if He finds us at His feet in adoration, disposing ourselves to receive Divine favours. No sooner had Saul of Tarsus, the persecutor, humbled himself before his Maker than God sent a special messenger to his relief, telling him that 'even now he is at his prayers' (Acts 9:11). Even the person who has fallen can expect reassurance if he watches and prays.

    They shall increase, that hitherto had dwindled, be exalted, that once were brought low. (Jer. 30:19, 20)

8. Because the Holy Hour is a personal prayer, the person who limits himself strictly to his official obligation is like the union man who downs tools the moment the whistle blows. Love begins when duty finishes. It is a giving of the cloak when the coat is taken. It is walking the extra mile.

Answer shall come ere cry for help is uttered; prayer find audience while it is yet on their lips. (Isa. 65:24)

Of course, we do not have to make a Holy Hour – and that is just the point. Love is never compelled, except in hell. Their love has to submit to justice. To be forced to love would be a kind of hell. No man who loves a woman is obligated to give her an engagement ring, and no person who loves the Sacred Heart ever has to give an engagement Hour.

"Would you, too, go away?" (John 6:68) is weak love; "Art thou sleeping?" (Mark 14:37) is irresponsible love; "He had great possessions" (Matt. 19:22; Mark 10:22) is selfish love. But does the person who loves His Lord have time for other activities before he performs acts of love "above and beyond the call of duty"? Does the patient love the physician who charges for every call, or does he begin to love when the physician says, "I just dropped by to see how you were"?

9. Meditation keeps us from seeking an external escape from our worries and miseries. When difficulties arise, when nerves are made taut by false accusations, there is always a danger that we may look outwards, as the Israelites did, for release.

From the Lord God, the Holy One of Israel, word was given to you, Come back and keep still, and all shall be well with you; in quietness and in confidence lies your strength. But you would have none of it; To horse! You cried We must flee! And flee you shall; We must ride swiftly, you said, but swifter still ride your pursuers. (Isa. 30:15, 16)

No outward escape, neither pleasure, drink, friends, nor keeping busy, is an answer. The soul cannot "fly upon a horse"; it must take "wings" to a place where its "life is hidden away ... with Christ in God" (Col. 3:3).

10. Finally, because the Holy Hour is necessary for the Church. No one can read the Old Testament without becoming

conscious of the presence of God in history. How often did God use other nations to punish Israel for her sins? He made Assyria the "rod that executes my vengeance" (Isa.. 10:5). The history of the world since the Incarnation is the Way of the Cross. The rise of nations and their fall remain related to the Kingdom of God. We cannot understand the mystery of God's government, for it is the "sealed book" of the Apocalypse. John wept when he saw it (Rev. 5:4). He could not understand why this moment of prosperity and that hour of adversity.

The sole requirement is the venture of faith, and the reward is the depths of intimacy for those who cultivate His friendship. To abide with Christ is spiritual fellowship, as He insisted on the solemn and sacred night of the Last Supper, the moment He chose to give us the Eucharist:

You have only to live on in me, and I will live on in you. (John 15:4)

He wants us in His dwelling: That you, too, may be where I am. (John 14:3)

How to Make a Holy Hour

"Let nothing hinder thee from praying always and be not afraid to be justified even to death for the rewards of God continue forever. Before prayer prepare thy soul; and be not as a man that tempt God"

— (Sir. 18; 22-23).

Prayer is the lifting of our soul to God, unto the end of perfectly corresponding to His Holy Will. Our Divine Lord, describing His Mission, said: "For I have come down from heaven, not to do my own will, but the will of him who sent me ... the Father, that I should lose nothing of what he has given me, but that I should raise it up on the

35

last day" (John 6:38, 39). "My food is to do the will of him who sent me, to accomplish his work" (John 4:34).

To correspond to the Divine Will, we must, first of all, know it, and secondly, have the grace and strength to correspond with it, once it is known. But to attain these two gifts of light for our minds and power for our wills, we must live on terms of intimate friendship with God. This is done through prayer. A prayerful life is, therefore, one lived in conformity with the Holy Will of God, as a prayerless life is a life of self-will and selfishness.

There is an element of prayer common to Jews, Protestants, and Catholics, namely, belief in God. Above half of the prayers, for example, which a priest says in his Divine Office, are taken from the Old Testament. In relation to all three, that is, Jews, Protestants, and Catholics, a Holy Hour will, therefore, be understood as one Hour a day spent in meditating on God and our eternal salvation. This Holy Hour can be made anywhere.

For Catholics, however, the Holy Hour has a very special significance. It means a continuous and unbroken Hour spent in the presence of Our Divine Lord in the Eucharist; for which reason, a meditation on the Blessed Eucharist has been included as one of these meditations in this book.

In the case of priests and religious, it is suggested that they make this Holy Hour in addition to their usual recitation of the Divine Office and Holy Mass.

This Holy Hour will be spent in prayer and meditation. A distinction is here made between the two, with the emphasis on the latter. By prayer, we here understand the recitation of formal prayers, generally composed by a person different from him who prays.

The Psalms represent one of the highest forms of vocal prayer and are common to Jews, Protestants, and Catholics. Other vocal prayers include the Our Father, Hail Mary, Creed, Confiteor, Acts of Faith, Hope, and Charity, and thousands of other prayers found in religious books. There are three kinds of attention in vocal prayer: (1) to the words, lest we say them wrong; (2) to their sense and meaning; and (3) to God and the intention for which we pray. The last kind of attention is essential to vocal prayer.

But the principal purpose of these Holy Hour meditations is the cultivation of mental prayer or meditation. Very few souls ever meditate; they are either frightened by the word or else never taught its existence. In the human order, a person in love is always conscious of the one loved, lives in the presence of the other, resolves to do the will of the other, and regards as his greatest jealousy being outdone in the least advantage of self-giving. Apply this to a soul in love with God, and you have the rudiments of meditation.

Meditation is, therefore, a kind of communing of spirit with spirit, with God as its object. Without attempting to set down the formal aspects of meditation, but to make it as intelligible as possible to beginners, the technique of meditation is as follows:

1. We speak to God: We begin by putting ourselves in the presence of God. For those who make the Holy Hour before the Blessed Sacrament, there must be a consciousness of our presence before the Body, Blood, Soul, and Divinity of Our Lord and Saviour Jesus Christ. Naturally, there are varying degrees of intimacy with persons. In a theatre, there are hundreds present, but little or no intimacy between them. The intimacy deepens to the degree that we establish conversation with one or more of them, and according as this conversation springs from a common interest. So it is with God.

   Prayer, then, is not a mere asking for things, but an aiming at a transformation; that is, a becoming "conformed to the image of his Son" (Rom. 8:29). We pray not to dispose God to give us something, but to dispose ourselves to receive something from Him: the fullness of Divine Life.

2. God speaks to us: Activity is not only on the human side but also on the Divine. A conversation is an exchange, not a

monologue. As the soul willed to draw near God, God wills to draw near the soul. It would be wrong to monopolize the conversation with friends; it is more wrong to do so in our relations with God. We must not do all the talking; we must also be good listeners. "Speak Lord, for thy servant heareth" (1 Kings 3:9).

The soul now experiences the truth of the words "Draw near to God, and he will draw near to you" (James 4:8). All during the meditation, it will conceive devout affections of adoration, petition, sacrifice, and reparation to God, but particularly at the close of the meditation. These affections or colloquies are to be offered preferably in our own language, for every soul must make its own love to God, and God loves each soul in a particular manner.

"In the beginning, the soul attracted to Jesus by some impulse of grace comes to Him, filled with natural thoughts and aspirations, and very ignorant of the supernatural. It understands neither God nor itself. It has a few intimate relations with the Divinity outside of itself and within itself, but it begins to converse with Jesus. If it persists in the frequentation of His company, the Lord gradually takes an ever-increasing share in the conversation and begins to enlighten the soul.

In its contemplation of the mysteries of faith, He aids it to penetrate beneath the words and facts and symbols, hitherto known but superficially, and to grasp the inner sense of the supernatural truths contained in these facts or words or symbols. The Scriptures are gradually opened to the soul. The well-known texts begin to acquire a new and deeper meaning. Familiar expressions convey a knowledge, which the soul wonders never to have before discovered in them. All this new light is directed towards giving a fuller and more perfect comprehension of the mysteries of our faith, which are the mysteries of the life of Jesus" (Leen, Progress Through Mental Prayer, p. 29. Sheed & Ward).

Do not read these meditations as a story. Read a few lines slowly; close the book; think about the truth contained in them; apply them to your own life; speak to God about how little you have corresponded to His Will, how anxious you are to do it; listen to God speaking to your soul; make acts of faith, hope, and love to God, and only when that train of thought has been exhausted should you proceed to the next idea. A single Holy Hour will not necessarily require reading a chapter of this book. If one meditates well, a single chapter should provide thoughts for many Holy Hours.

When this book of meditations is exhausted, take up either the Sacred Scriptures or some truly spiritual book, or the life of a saint, and use it for inspiration and for meditation.

How to Begin Your Own Holy Hour of Reparation

The Holy Hour is not just a pious tradition — it is a powerful act of love and reparation. Archbishop Fulton J. Sheen called it 'the hour that makes the day holy.' St. Thérèse of Lisieux lived her own Holy Hours hidden in the cloister, offering little things with great love. The invitation is now extended to you.

Whether you are able to spend time before the Blessed Sacrament in a chapel or pray from home in spiritual communion, you can begin your own Holy Hour of Reparation with simple steps, intentional love, and quiet fidelity.

Suggested Structure for a Holy Hour

1. Begin with Silence (5 minutes) – Gaze upon the Holy Face of Christ. Ask for the grace to see Him in His sorrow, His silence, and His love.

2. Act of Contrition – Offer reparation for your sins and the sins of the world. You may pray: "O my Jesus, I am sorry for having offended You. I desire to console Your Heart."

3. Meditate on Scripture (10–15 minutes) – Choose one passage from the appendix or another Gospel scene. Let the words enter slowly. Listen.

4. Spiritual Reading (optional) – Read a short meditation or quote from St. Thérèse or Fulton Sheen. Let it echo silently in your heart.

5. Rosary or Chaplet of the Holy Face – Offer one of the prayers of reparation. Unite your intercessions to the wounds of Christ.

6. Quiet Adoration or Gaze (15 minutes) – Simply remain with Him. No need for many words. Be present. Be still. Be His.

7. Closing Prayer of Surrender – Offer a final prayer: "Jesus, may I never turn away from Your Face. Receive my heart as a veil of love and reparation."

Remember:

Your fidelity is more important than your feelings. A short, sincere Holy Hour done with love consoles Christ far more than lengthy words spoken without the heart. Begin where you are. Offer what you have. He will do the rest.

CONCLUDING WORD

Sent from Lisieux

At the heart of this little way shines the Holy Face of Christ. It is a Face marred by suffering yet radiant with love, a silent Gospel that invites us to trust, to offer, to surrender. St. Thérèse teaches us that sanctity does not lie in great deeds but in small acts of love performed with great fidelity. And Fulton Sheen reminds us that in contemplating the Holy Face, every tear, every sacrifice, every hidden offering becomes a seed of redemption.

As you close these pages, may you open your heart to the Face of Jesus, and through daily fidelity to love, allow Him to engrave His likeness upon your soul. The world awaits saints made luminous by His countenance. Let us go forth, then, carrying the imprint of His Face, and living the Little Way of trust and surrender.

Behold Your Mother

Mary, the Cross, and the Power of Reparation

A SHEEN MISSION SERIES VOLUME II

BEHOLD YOUR MOTHER

Mary, the Cross, and the Power of Reparation.
A Mission of Consolation, Intimacy, and Devotion.
A Sheen Mission Series - Volume II

The Sheen Mission Series invites you to walk with Archbishop Fulton J. Sheen in prayer, reparation, and renewal — a journey of the Holy Face, the Cross, the Eucharist and Our Blessed Mother.

Description:

*B*ehold Your Mother is the second volume in the Sheen Mission Series — a Marian companion for those who wish to walk more closely with Our Lady at the foot of the Cross.

Here you will discover meditations on the Seven Sorrows of Mary, reflections on her role in salvation history, and the consoling strength she offers to those who suffer. With Archbishop Fulton Sheen as a guide, this volume invites you to enter into Mary's tender care and to experience her love as Mother and Queen.

> *"When Jesus said to John, 'Behold your mother,' He gave us His Mother to be ours. No one can ever say that he is alone in the world when he has Mary as his Mother."*
>
> **— Archbishop Fulton J. Sheen**

FOREWORD

*"To a great extent, the level of any civilization
is the level of its womanhood."*

— **Archbishop Fulton J. Sheen**

In every age, the Blessed Virgin Mary has stood as the model of purity, love, and sacrifice. And in our time — a time of wounded hearts and weary souls — she shines all the more brightly. This book is a call to return to her embrace, to listen anew to her sorrows, and to join her in the work of reparation.

When Archbishop Fulton J. Sheen spoke of the Blessed Virgin Mary, he did not speak merely of doctrine or sentiment. He spoke of a *Person*. He loved her with the fire of a son and the reverence of a priest. He once said, "She is the one whom every man loves when he loves a woman,". For Sheen, Mary was not only the Mother of God — she was the Mother of us all. At the foot of the Cross, mysteriously, she became our co-sufferer, our co-redeemer, and the spiritual Mother of every soul who longs for Heaven.

This book — the second volume in this mission series — is born from the pulpit, the confessional, and the quiet tears of countless souls who have knelt before the image of the Sorrowful Mother. It is a pilgrimage in print: a retreat with Mary at the foot of the Cross.

These meditations draw from parish missions, Marian devotions, and the theology of saints like St. Louis de Montfort, St. Alphonsus Liguori, and St. Therese of the Child Jesus. But above all, they echo the voice of Sheen — who taught us that Calvary is not just a place to witness, but a place to join.

Let Mary take your hand. Let her lead you back to the Heart of her Son. And as she whispers in your soul: *"Behold, your mother"* — may you echo back, *"Behold, my love."*

INTRODUCTION

Why Mary? Why Now?

At the heart of every true renewal in the Church, there is always a woman. Not just any woman — but *the* Woman. The one clothed with the sun. The one whose "yes" changed the course of human history. The one who stood at the foot of the Cross and silently offered her Son back to the Father for the salvation of souls.

Today, the world is aching. Families are broken. Confusion reigns. And the Church — bruised but beloved — stands again at Calvary. Now more than ever, we must behold our Mother.

This is not a poetic suggestion. It is a divine command. *"Behold your mother,"* Jesus said from the Cross — not just to John, but to you, to me, to the Church across time. And in that moment, Mary's motherhood extended to every soul redeemed by the Blood of her Son. She became our comfort, our intercessor, and our companion in suffering.

But why now?

Because this is an age of war — a spiritual war waged not only in culture, but in hearts. And Mary has always been Heaven's secret weapon. She is the one the devil fears most. She crushes the serpent's head — not with might, but with humility; not with argument, but with love.

To return to Mary is not to flee from Christ, but to draw closer to Him. She is the shortcut to holiness, the mirror of His mercy, and the safest refuge for sinners. St. Maximilian Kolbe said, "Never be afraid of loving the Blessed Virgin too much," and "You can never love her more than Jesus did."

This book is not just another collection of meditations. It is an invitation to reparation. A call to console the Hearts of Jesus and Mary — pierced for our sins, yet ablaze with love. It is an opportunity to make your life a Marian offering. To walk the Way of the Cross with her. To see your own wounds reflected in her Sorrows. And to discover, in the silence of her gaze, the strength to carry your own cross.

We live in prophetic times. Times when the triumph of the Immaculate Heart is not merely a promise for the future, but a mission for the present.

May these pages draw you to her side. May they lead you to ponder her sorrows, imitate her courage, and live in the shadow of her maternal love. And as you journey through each reflection, may you hear the whispered invitation that echoes from Calvary:

"Behold your mother."

MEDITATION 1

The Prophecy of Simeon
– A Sword Shall Pierce

And Simeon blessed them and said to Mary his mother, "Behold, this child is set for the fall and rising of many in Israel, and for a sign that is spoken against — (and a sword will pierce through your own soul also), that thoughts out of many hearts may be revealed."

—Luke 2:34–35

The crib and the Cross were never far apart. In the arms of Mary, the Infant Jesus was adored as the Prince of Peace — but in the shadow of Simeon's words, He was already marked as the Man of Sorrows.

This first sorrow of Our Lady is not soaked in blood, yet it is sharp. A sword — invisible, prophetic, and real — is announced. Not for Christ, but for *her*. And this sword, unlike a Roman blade, will not wound the body — it will slice through the heart.

In the Temple, Mary receives more than a blessing. She receives a mission. She is told that her joy in this Child will become sorrow. That the light she holds will also reveal darkness. That her soul, so pure and hidden, will become the mirror in which the drama of redemption is reflected.

The sword is not just pain — it is participation. Mary is being invited into her Son's sufferings. She does not recoil. She does not protest. She receives this word in silence, just as she once received the angel's greeting: *Fiat*.

Archbishop Fulton Sheen once observed that "Mary is the only mother who ever knew she gave birth to a victim." The mystery of Christ's redemptive mission was not revealed to her all at once — but this moment, in the arms of Simeon, begins to unveil it. A sword awaits. And yet, she loves.

In that moment, Mary became the Mother of Sorrows.

A Mother's Heart

To suffer in the body is one thing. To suffer in the heart of a mother is another. Mary's sorrows are not merely emotional; they are *intercessory*. Her pierced soul allows her to enter into the pain of all her children.

Sheen once said, "No one can live without tears unless they have never loved." And Mary loved perfectly. Her heart was open, exposed, undefended — because her love was pure. That is what made the sword pierce so deeply.

The piercing of Mary's heart reveals something to us: that love and suffering are not opposites. In fact, the deepest love is often the most wounded. But those wounds become fountains of grace. Mary's pierced heart is now a refuge for all broken hearts.

For the Fall and Rise of Many

Simeon speaks of contradiction. He declares that Jesus will be opposed — and so too will His followers. The way of the Cross is never a straight, painless line. It invites a fall — a dying to pride, sin, and self. But it also offers a rising — a resurrection of the soul.

Mary stands at the threshold of this mystery. She accepts that her life will be marked by sorrow, not in despair, but in union with the redeeming plan of God. Her soul becomes a chalice, filled with the pain of the world and the love of the Redeemer.

A Call to Reparation

To meditate on this sorrow is to accept a sword of our own — the sword of compassion, of intercession, of co-suffering. We are invited to stand with Mary in the Temple, to receive the prophecy, and to not turn away.

Her sorrow is not sterile. It is fruitful. And it calls forth a response.

Will you let your own heart be pierced? Will you join her in reparation?

In a world where love is cheap and suffering is avoided, Mary stands as the contradiction. She embraces both.

Let us learn from her how to suffer with grace — and how to love with wounds.

MEDITATION 2

The Flight into Egypt
– A Mother's Protection in Exile

> *Now, when they had departed, behold, an angel of the Lord appeared to Joseph in a dream and said, "Rise, take the child and his mother, and flee to Egypt, and remain there till I tell you; for Herod is about to search for the child, to destroy him."*
>
> **— Matthew 2:13**

The stillness of Bethlehem is shattered by a warning in the night. There is no time to linger. No farewell. No comfort. The Holy Family, newly formed, must become a family in flight — not toward triumph, but into exile.

In the second sorrow of Our Lady, we see a maternal heart full of courage, obedience, and love. She who bore the Light of the world is now forced to flee from darkness. A tyrant wants her Son dead. And so, under cover of night, she sets off — not with fear, but with faith.

Mary does not argue with God. She does not resist the path laid before her. She protects the Child by trusting the Father. And in doing so, she teaches us what it means to guard the Christ-life in our own souls — especially in a world that often seeks to destroy it.

Archbishop Fulton Sheen once noted, *"The modern flight into Egypt takes place when truth is banished from the hearts of men."* In that light, Mary's flight is not just historical — it's mystical. It continues today. Every soul that carries Jesus must make this flight into interior exile, away from sin and toward the Father's will.

The Hidden Heroism of Mothers

The Gospels give us few details of the journey — no distances, no landscapes, no complaints. But what we do know is this: Mary was not simply a mother in distress. She was a mother on a mission.

The dangers were real — robbers, deserts, cold, thirst, uncertainty. But the presence of the Child made every hardship holy. What mother, upon holding the Saviour close, would not give everything for Him?

Mary is the model of mothers who must raise children in difficult times — in spiritual exile, amid moral confusion, under attack from a culture of death. She shows us that the real heroism of motherhood is not found in applause but in quiet sacrifice, made for the sake of protecting what is most sacred.

A Journey of Reparation

Why must the Saviour flee? Why must the Holy Family suffer?

Because even as a Child, Christ is entering into our human condition — the chaos, the evil, the unjust systems. He is the Divine Exile. And Mary, united with Him, begins to offer reparation not just for Herod's cruelty, but for all sin that tries to snuff out divine life.

This is the spiritual meaning of the Flight into Egypt: the refusal to allow the holy to be compromised. The flight is not cowardice; it is fidelity. Mary teaches us when to stand firm and when to flee — not from fear, but from evil.

There are seasons when reparation looks like confrontation. And there are times when it looks like retreat — retreat to prayer, hiddenness, silence. Mary's exile was not wasted time. It was a furnace of love, forged in fidelity.

You, Too, Must Flee

Today, there are many Herods. They come not with swords, but with seductions. They don't burn churches; they distract hearts. They make the soul numb and complacent. And so we are called, like Mary and Joseph, to *flee* — not physically, but spiritually.

To flee from pride.

To flee from impurity.

To flee from anything that would endanger the Christ-life within us.

And we flee not in panic — but in purpose.

Mary is the first of the exiles. The first of the hidden victims. And in her exile, she was never alone. She had the Child. She had Joseph. And above all, she had the will of the Father guiding every step.

Let us journey with her, not only in comfort, but in the desert — where true love is proven, and the soul learns how to make every step an act of reparation.

MEDITATION 3

The Loss of the Child Jesus
– When God Hides in Silence

And when they saw him, they were astonished; and his mother said to him, "Son, why have you treated us so? Behold, your father and I have been looking for you anxiously."

— Luke 2:48

There are few scenes in Scripture more human, more relatable, than this: a mother searching for her lost Child. For three days, Mary and Joseph looked for Jesus, hearts aching with each hour. And when they finally found Him — in the temple, speaking with doctors of the law — her words echoed the cry of every parent, every soul: *Why?*

This sorrow pierces deeply. It is not the suffering of persecution or exile. It is the anguish of silence — the hiddenness of God. Mary, who had never sinned, experiences the pain of not knowing where her Son is. She represents the soul in darkness, the believer in desolation.

Archbishop Fulton Sheen once said, *"It is in the darkness that we find God — the darkness of faith, not of despair."* Mary teaches us that faith endures even when God seems absent. Her sorrow was not a lack of belief — it was the ache of love.

The Silence of the Saints

Saint Thérèse of Lisieux, in her final illness, confessed that her faith was tested not by sin, but by *God's silence*. She, too, lost the sense of His nearness. She, too, cried out in the night. Yet like Mary, she clung to Him with love, not understanding.

There is a silence that purifies. A silence that strips us of superficial devotions, empty feelings, and spiritual pride. In this silence, the soul is asked one question: *Do you love Me still?*

Mary's yes — even in her confusion — teaches us to remain. To search. To keep walking, even when the road grows cold.

Reparation in the Dark

There is a great mystery in this third sorrow: that the One who is Wisdom Itself allows His mother to suffer for love of Him. He does not prevent the loss. He permits it — not out of cruelty, but to deepen her heart.

Reparation is not always about doing. Sometimes it is about *bearing* — bearing the absence, the dryness, the unknowing. These are hidden sufferings, invisible to the world, but precious to God.

To suffer for Christ is holy.

But to suffer from Christ — and still love Him — is divine.

Mary teaches us how to offer the pain of confusion as reparation. She shows us how to pray even when we do not feel God's presence. She is the companion of every soul that walks through the night of faith.

Finding Him Again

When Mary finds Jesus, she does not scold. She questions — gently, sorrowfully — but she does not rebuke the divine plan. And He, in turn, speaks a mystery: *"Did you not know I must be about My Father's business?"*

It is a strange comfort. Not an explanation. But a reminder: that even in absence, Jesus is working. Even when we do not feel Him, He is still fulfilling the Father's will.

Mary pondered all these things in her heart. So must we.

If you feel like you've lost Him —

If your prayers are dry, your soul confused —

If heaven seems quiet and your heart aches with longing —

Then this sorrow is yours.

And so is Mary.

Let her lead you back. Not by sight, but by faith. For in the finding — there is not just relief — but a deeper, truer love.

MEDITATION 4

Mary Meets Jesus on the Way of the Cross – Love That Does Not Turn Away

> *And there followed him a great multitude of the people, and of women, who bewailed and lamented him.*
>
> **— Luke 23:27**

No words are recorded between them. No miracles worked. No comfort given.

Just a meeting.

A mother and her Son, locked in a gaze through sweat, blood, and tears, amidst the cruelty of the crowd. On the road to Calvary, Mary does not faint. She does not beg for mercy. She stands. She walks. She *meets* her Son.

And He, bruised and beaten, looks up through swollen eyes... and sees her.

In that moment, love is exchanged without words. A mother's silent yes meets a Son's saving yes. And a sword, once prophesied by Simeon, now cuts deeper than ever.

The Strength of the Mother

Many imagine Mary as frail and soft, but the Gospels show something different. She is strong — strong enough to stand by a condemned Son when others fled. Strong enough to bear witness to His agony. Strong enough to walk with Him, even when it meant walking into suffering.

Archbishop Fulton Sheen wrote:

> *"It was not a woman who fled at the garden, nor a woman who denied Him at the fire. It was not a woman who stood not beneath the Cross… it was a woman who was faithful."*

Mary's strength is not loud or showy. It is the strength of presence — the power of staying.

She did not stop the Cross. She shared it.

The Power of Compassion

The word "compassion" means *to suffer with*. On the road to Calvary, Mary models this perfectly. She does not take Jesus' pain away — she enters it.

In your own life, you will encounter crosses — your own and those of others. Mary's example calls us not to flee, not to fix everything, but to *be present*. To walk with those in sorrow. To love in the midst of pain.

That is reparation: not simply atonement for sin, but love poured out where love was once denied.

When Suffering Meets Suffering

This fourth sorrow is a school of love. Not the love of poetry or sentiment, but of sacrifice. Here we see what it means to love when nothing can be done — except to be near.

Have you met someone on their road of suffering?

Have you stood by a loved one through illness, addiction, loss, or despair?

Have you looked into the eyes of someone you cannot save... and stayed?

Then you know something of this sorrow. You know something of Mary's heart.

Reparation through Presence

Our world fears pain. It turns away from the broken, the dying, the inconvenient. But Mary does not look away. And neither must we.

If we want to console the Heart of Jesus, we must walk His path. We must enter into the mystery of the Cross — not alone, but with Mary.

Stay close to her.

Let her teach you to love without needing answers.

Let her show you that even the smallest act of presence — a hand held, a tear shared, a gaze of love — can redeem.

For when suffering meets suffering in love, Heaven draws near.

MEDITATION 5

The Crucifixion
– Standing at the Foot of the Cross

So the soldiers did this. But standing by the cross of Jesus were his mother, and his mother's sister, Mary the wife of Clopas, and Mary Magdalene.

— John 19:25

It is the most sacred ground in history — Calvary.

And there, as the world looked away in horror, Mary *stood*.

She stood in sorrow, not collapse.

She stood in silence, not protest.

She stood in surrender, not despair.

The Blessed Virgin Mary did not fall at the Cross. She stood *with* the Cross. She stood *under* the Cross. She stood as the Church's first co-sufferer and our model of courageous love.

The Priest and the Woman

As the High Priest offered Himself on the altar of the Cross, a woman offered her heart. Her presence was not incidental; it was integral. She who gave Him flesh now watched that flesh torn apart. She who nursed the infant Christ now beheld Him pierced.

Archbishop Fulton Sheen once wrote:

> *"Mary at the foot of the Cross is the model of what our attitude should be toward Calvary. She is not a hysterical woman with disheveled hair and sobbing uncontrollably. She is a strong woman — a queen among women — a queen among martyrs."*

Her heart did not break from hopelessness. It broke from love. And that love became the seedbed of reparation.

Behold Your Mother

Only one sentence is recorded from Mary at Calvary — and it is not spoken by her.

It is spoken *to* her.

> *"Woman, behold, your son!" Then he said to the disciple, "Behold, your mother!"*
>
> **— John 19:26-27**

In that moment, Mary became more than the Mother of Christ — she became the Mother of the Church. The beloved disciple, traditionally understood as John, represents each of us. And to him — to us — Christ entrusts His Mother.

We are not orphans.

We are not alone.

We have been given the greatest advocate and consoler: the Mother of Sorrows.

The Silent Offering

At the foot of the Cross, Mary says nothing. But her silence is not absence. It is *consent*. She offers her Son to the Father, just as she once offered Him in the temple. The world crucifies — she consents. The world mocks — she loves.

This is the heart of reparation: not to undo the world's evil, but to *offer* love in the face of it.

Reparation is not passive. It is deeply active — but the action is interior. It is the prayerful union of our suffering with Christ's. It is the soul whispering, "Fiat," even when the world says, "Crucify."

Our Own Calvaries

There are crosses we are called to *stand beneath*, not run from:

- The sickness of a spouse

- The rebellion of a child

- The grief of a buried dream

- The weight of unanswered prayers

Mary shows us how to stand — not angrily, not hopelessly, but *faithfully*.

She teaches us that presence is power. That fidelity is fruitfulness. That Calvary, endured in union with Christ, is not the end — it is the beginning of Resurrection.

The Call to Stand

To stand at the Cross is to be Catholic.

To stand at the Cross is to be Marian.

To stand at the Cross is to become like Mary: a soul pierced but not defeated.

So stand.

Stand when it's hard.

Stand when it's quiet.

Stand when the world calls you foolish.

For there, at the foot of the Cross, you will find Mary...

And where Mary stands, Heaven is not far behind.

MEDITATION 6

The Gift of a Mother – Marian Love and the Healing of Souls

"If we do not become children, we cannot enter the Kingdom of Heaven. If we do not become Marian, we cannot understand Christ."

— **Archbishop Fulton J. Sheen**

At the Cross, Jesus gave us His Mother.

He didn't give us doctrine, ritual, or rules — He gave us Mary.

And in doing so, He gave us the most tender path to healing.

Love that Heals

Marian love is not a sentimental devotion. It is a *healing encounter*. Mary's love heals not by replacing the Cross, but by guiding us through it. She walks with the wounded. She consoles the broken. She mothers the sinners.

Her heart — immaculate and pierced — has room for every soul.

Just as she wrapped the Christ-Child in swaddling clothes, she now wraps us in the folds of her mantle. She does not take away suffering. She walks us into the fire — and out of it — as only a mother can.

Reparation Is Womb-Like

Reparation in union with Mary becomes a *birthing place* of grace. She teaches us to suffer not with bitterness but with fruitfulness.

Think of the womb: silent, hidden, sacrificial. A mother's body makes space for another — and in doing so, she co-creates life.

This is Marian reparation.

We create space in our hearts to carry the pain of others. We make of our trials a tabernacle. And in silence, in surrender, in trust — love is born again.

The Devotion of the Little Ones

St. Thérèse of Lisieux, child of Mary and Doctor of the Church, called Mary "more Mother than Queen." For St. Thérèse, it was the *simplicity* of Mary that made her powerful. Mary was not distant or unapproachable, but tender, motherly, and near.

St. Thérèse wrote:

"She is so simple, that one cannot fear her."

Do you fear approaching God?

Are you ashamed of your past, your wounds, your weakness?

Go to Mary.

She will not turn you away. She will teach you to walk the Little Way — a path of confidence, childlike surrender, and humble trust.

The Mission of a Mother

Every soul wounded by sin is a soul waiting to be mothered. Every person drifting in spiritual confusion is silently aching for a maternal hand. And every Church — even in her majesty and sacraments — needs the tenderness of a Mother to be complete.

Mary is not a footnote in salvation history. She is the living heart of the Church.

To be Marian is to become fully alive.

To be Marian is to know how to suffer well.

To be Marian is to receive love so deeply that we cannot help but give it away.

Entrustment and Healing

When we entrust our pain to Mary, we do not lose it — we *offer* it. She gathers our broken pieces and places them, like little flowers, at the foot of the Cross.

And there, with tears and trust, Heaven transforms them.

So go ahead — bring your wounds to the Mother.

- Bring your guilt.

- Bring your fatigue.

- Bring your unspoken ache.

She will not condemn.

She will not reject.

She will carry you as she carried Christ — all the way to the Resurrection.

MEDITATION 7

The Immaculate Heart and the Wounded Heart

In every image of Our Lady of Sorrows, we see two hearts in profound dialogue — her Immaculate Heart, pure and sinless, and the Wounded Heart of her Son, pierced for our salvation. This mystery is not only artistic but deeply theological: the two hearts beat in unison, sharing the same love for the Father, the same sorrow for sin, and the same longing for our redemption.

Mary's Heart was fashioned to be the perfect echo of Jesus' Heart. If His Sacred Heart burned with divine charity, hers burned with maternal charity. If His Heart was pierced by the lance on Calvary, hers was pierced mystically at that very moment by a sword foretold by Simeon. She did not merely witness His Passion; she interiorly suffered it with Him. This co-suffering, called *compassio* by the saints, is not a claim of equality with the Redeemer, but of intimate participation in His work.

Archbishop Fulton Sheen often spoke of Mary as "the only one who truly understood the cost of our salvation." She had no illusions about the price of sin. She held the Innocent Lamb at Bethlehem; she watched Him grow in wisdom and stature; she saw Him rejected by the very ones He came to save. And then she stood at the foot of the Cross — the place where the price was fully paid.

St. Thérèse of Lisieux, though so tender in her love for the Child Jesus, also grasped the sorrow of Mary. In her simple yet profound way, she wrote:

"Mary is more Mother than Queen; her glory is not in power but in tenderness, not in majesty but in mercy."

Mary's compassion was not a passing sentiment; it was the fruit of perfect love. She teaches us that to truly love Christ means to suffer with Him and for Him. The Immaculate Heart beats for sinners, not because sin is light, but because grace is greater. Her maternal mission did not end at Calvary — it intensified. From the Cross, Jesus entrusted John to Mary and Mary to John. In that moment, she became Mother to every disciple.

The woundedness of her Heart is, paradoxically, the source of her power. The devil fears Mary because she shares so perfectly in the victory of her Son. Her Immaculate Heart is a refuge for the repentant, a fortress for the weak, and a beacon for the wandering. Devotion to her Heart is not a sentimental exercise but a school of sacrificial love.

To honor the Immaculate Heart is to join Mary in contemplating the wounds of Jesus — not with cold observation, but with loving participation. We place our hearts within hers so that she may shape them according to the Heart of her Son. And in this exchange, we learn to say with her: "Behold the Handmaid of the Lord; be it done unto me according to thy word."

MEDITATION 8

Mary at the Foot of the Cross: The School of Love and Suffering

No scene in all of human history reveals the depth of love and the cost of redemption more than Calvary. At the foot of the Cross stands Mary, the Mother of Jesus, steadfast and silent, her soul pierced with the sword foretold by Simeon. It is here, in this hour of darkness, that she becomes for us the model of unwavering faith, total surrender, and selfless love.

Archbishop Fulton Sheen often remarked that *"Mary's greatest moment was not in Bethlehem when she gave birth to Christ, but on Calvary when she gave Him up."* In Bethlehem, she offered Him her body; on Calvary, she offered Him her heart. Here we enter the mystery of the union between a Mother's love and a Redeemer's mission.

The Gaze of the Mother

The Gospels give us no recorded words from Mary at the Cross. Her silence speaks more loudly than any speech. Her eyes were fixed on Jesus, absorbing His pain into her heart, uniting her soul with His sacrifice. She did not turn away. She did not despair. Her steadfast presence teaches us the ministry of accompaniment — to be present with those who suffer, even when we cannot remove their pain.

In our own trials, how often do we look away from the Cross, seeking easier paths? Mary's gaze invites us to remain — to stand at the place of suffering with courage and fidelity. To see with her eyes is to see suffering through the lens of love.

The Gift of Spiritual Motherhood

From the Cross, Jesus utters words that change the course of salvation history: *"Woman, behold your son."* And to St. John: *"Behold your mother."* In that moment, Mary becomes the Mother of all the redeemed. She takes into her heart every soul purchased by the Blood of Christ. Fulton Sheen notes that Mary's spiritual motherhood is not a vague sentiment, but a deep participation in the redemptive mission of her Son. She mothers us into holiness, nurturing Christ's life in our souls.

The School of Love and Suffering

To stand with Mary at the Cross is to enroll in the school of love and suffering. Here we learn that love without sacrifice is shallow, and suffering without love is unbearable. In her school, suffering becomes fruitful when united to Christ's Passion. She teaches us to offer our pain — whether physical, emotional, or spiritual — as a gift to God for the salvation of souls.

Saint Thérèse of Lisieux, who bore the title *"of the Child Jesus and the Holy Face"*, learned this Marian lesson well. Her "little way" was filled with small sacrifices offered with great love, echoing Mary's quiet yet powerful "yes" beneath the Cross.

Remaining at the Foot of the Cross Today

Mary's example is not confined to history. In our own times of trial, we are called to "remain" with Christ in the Eucharist, in Adoration, and in prayer. To kneel at the tabernacle is to kneel at Calvary, where Mary still invites us to behold her Son and allow His love to transform us.

The world seeks comfort without cost, love without commitment, and faith without the Cross. Mary reminds us that there is no Easter Sunday without Good Friday. She leads us to embrace the Cross not as a sign of defeat, but as the tree of victory.

MEDITATION 9

Mary at the Foot of the Cross: The Perfect Model of Reparation

The Gospels tell us that "standing by the cross of Jesus were His mother, and His mother's sister, Mary the wife of Clopas, and Mary Magdalene" (John 19:25). At the most excruciating moment in human history, when the weight of the world's sins bore down upon the Saviour, Mary did not turn away. She stood. She remained. She endured.

This standing was no passive stance. It was the posture of unwavering fidelity, of full union with the redemptive suffering of her Son. She was not merely present as an onlooker — Mary was actively participating in the offering of Christ to the Father. Every mother suffers when her child suffers; yet Mary's suffering was unique because she consented, with the deepest act of her will, to the sacrifice unfolding before her.

Saint John Paul II described her as "co-suffering" with Christ. This does not diminish the unique role of Jesus as the Redeemer — rather, it shows the depth of Mary's maternal union with Him. She accepted in advance the piercing of her own soul, prophesied by Simeon, and when it came, she embraced it as her share in the redemption of mankind.

Archbishop Fulton Sheen would often say that Mary's greatest title is not merely "Mother of God," but "Mother of the Redeemer." The difference is subtle yet profound. As "Mother of God," she gave Jesus His humanity. As "Mother of the Redeemer," she joined herself to His mission, offering her will, her love, and her suffering in complete harmony with His.

In the mystery of reparation, Mary becomes our teacher. She shows us that reparation is not simply saying prayers of apology for sin—it is uniting ourselves to Christ's sacrifice in such a way that our lives become an offering of love to the Father. This means standing with Jesus in the moments of darkness, humiliation, and abandonment, and choosing not to run from the Cross.

In our own lives, this can take many forms: standing by a suffering family member, refusing to abandon our faith in moments of trial, or offering our hidden sufferings in silence for souls in need. When we do so with Mary at our side, we share in her steadfast love and unshakable fidelity.

At Calvary, Mary became the spiritual mother of all who would follow her Son. From the Cross, Jesus entrusted her to John — and through John, to us. We who take her into our hearts are invited to share in her mission of bringing souls to Christ through the power of reparation.

Reflection Questions:

1) When have you felt called to "stand by the Cross" in your own life?

2) How can you imitate Mary's unwavering presence in the face of suffering?

3) What specific acts of reparation can you offer this week for the conversion of souls?

Prayer:

O Sorrowful Mother, who stood with courage and love beside your crucified Son, teach me to stand faithfully in the shadow of the Cross. May my life be a living act of reparation, united to the Heart of Jesus and to your Immaculate Heart. **Amen.**

MEDITATION 10

Mary at the Foot of the Cross: The Model of Perseverance in Suffering

The scene at Calvary is the ultimate classroom of love, perseverance, and faith.

Here, at the foot of the Cross, stands Mary — silent, steadfast, unyielding in her fidelity. While others fled, she remained. While many despaired, she trusted. In her heart, sorrow and faith met in a mysterious embrace.

St. John's Gospel gives us the briefest description:

> *Standing by the cross of Jesus were his mother, and his mother's sister, Mary the wife of Clopas, and Mary Magdalene*
>
> **— John 19:25**

The brevity of the verse almost hides the depth of the reality — but in that single image, the Church has found endless inspiration for centuries.

1. Perseverance: The Fruit of Love

Mary did not endure this suffering out of mere obligation; she remained because her love for God was greater than the pain of the moment. In this, she shows us that perseverance is not rooted in stoicism, but in love.

Fulton Sheen once said, "When *love enters the soul, pain no longer remains pain; it becomes sacrifice.*" Mary understood this truth perfectly.

2. The Silence of the Suffering

At Calvary, Mary's silence speaks volumes. She does not argue with the soldiers, nor cry out in protest. Her silence is not resignation, but a deep participation in the mystery unfolding before her eyes.

In our own trials, there are moments when silence becomes the most eloquent prayer — a silent offering of self to God.

3. A Call to Remain

In the spiritual life, perseverance is often the hardest virtue to maintain. It is easy to begin with enthusiasm; it is another thing entirely to remain faithful when the Cross becomes heavy. Mary teaches us to *remain* — not because the suffering is bearable, but because God is worthy.

When your spiritual journey brings you to your own Calvary — whether in illness, misunderstanding, loss, or spiritual dryness — remember Mary's example. She stayed, even when she could not fully see the glory that was to come.

4. The Gift She Received

At the Cross, Mary was entrusted with the whole human family through the words of Jesus:

> *"Woman, behold, your son!" Then he said to the disciple, "Behold, your mother!" And from that hour the disciple took her to his own home."*

— (John 19:26–27)

In persevering, she received a new mission — to be Mother to every disciple. This is the hidden blessing of remaining faithful: in our endurance, God often entrusts us with a deeper calling.

Reflection:

In moments of trial, ask Our Lady to help you stand with her at the foot of the Cross. Let her steadfastness inspire your own. The Cross is not the end — it is the doorway to Resurrection.

Prayer:

O Mary, faithful Mother, teach me to remain at the foot of my crosses with you. When I am tempted to flee, give me the courage to stay. When I am tempted to despair, whisper to my heart the hope of the Resurrection. **Amen.**

MEDITATION 11

The Compassion of Mary at the Foot of the Cross

No human heart has ever shared in the sufferings of Christ as deeply as the Immaculate Heart of His Mother. At Calvary, Mary stood— silent, steadfast, and sorrowful — bearing in her soul the full weight of her Son's agony. She did not cry out in despair, nor did she collapse in grief. She stood. And by standing, she revealed the strength of her faith and the depth of her love.

Saint John tells us simply: *"Standing by the Cross of Jesus was His Mother"* (John 19:25). That short phrase contains a world of meaning. Mary's presence was not a passive one. Her standing was an act of courage, an offering of herself in union with her Son's redemptive sacrifice. She was the New Eve at the side of the New Adam, sharing in the victory over sin and death.

Archbishop Fulton Sheen once said that Mary's greatest suffering was not the sword in her own heart, but watching the sword pierce the Heart of her Son. Every lash, every jeer, every drop of blood was felt in her soul. She was the most faithful disciple, the one who believed without seeing, who trusted even when all seemed lost.

Her compassion was not mere emotion—it was participation. In her, we see what it means to take up the Cross, to stand firm in faith when trials press in. The Church calls her *Co-Redemptrix* not because she adds to the work of Christ, but because she shares in it uniquely and completely, giving her maternal "Yes" even when it costs her everything.

For us, the lesson is clear: if we wish to draw near to Christ in His Passion, we must draw near to Mary. She teaches us how to suffer with love, how to unite our pain to His, and how to remain faithful in the darkest hour.

Reflection Question:

When I stand at the foot of the Cross—in my own trials or in those of others — do I waver, or do I remain steadfast with Mary?

Prayer:

O Mother of Sorrows, teach me to stand with you at the foot of the Cross, to love Jesus with a faithful heart, and to offer my own sufferings in union with His for the salvation of souls. **Amen.**

MEDITATION 12

The Seven Sorrows and the Power of Reparation

Mary's life was marked by joy, but also by a deep sharing in the sufferings of her Son. The Church, in her wisdom, has given us the devotion of the **Seven Sorrows of Mary** so we may meditate upon the mysteries that pierced her Immaculate Heart:

1) The Prophecy of Simeon

2) The Flight into Egypt

3) The Loss of the Child Jesus in the Temple

4) Meeting Jesus on the Way to Calvary

5) The Crucifixion and Death of Jesus

6) The Taking Down of the Body of Jesus from the Cross

7) The Burial of Jesus

Each sorrow is a window into the heart of the Mother of God. In everyone, she responds not with resentment but with love, accepting the will of the Father even when it is shrouded in mystery and pain.

In meditating on her sorrows, we enter into the school of reparation. Mary teaches us how to atone — not by adding to Christ's sacrifice, but by uniting ourselves to it with love. Fulton Sheen wrote: *"The closer one gets to Mary, the more one sees that her life was a continual Calvary."*

Reparation is not simply making amends; it is love's response to wounded love. Our sins have wounded the Heart of Jesus, and through Him, the Heart of Mary. By offering our prayers, sacrifices, and daily crosses in union with hers, we participate in the healing work of grace.

One of the most fruitful ways to live this devotion is to set aside time each week — especially on Fridays — to meditate upon the Seven Sorrows. As we do, we find that Mary's sorrows are not sources of despair, but of hope, because they lead directly to the Resurrection.

Reflection Question:

How can I imitate Mary's faith in times of sorrow so that my suffering becomes a prayer of love?

Prayer:

O Mother most sorrowful, obtain for me the grace to unite my heart to yours, that I may console the Heart of your Son and help bring souls to His mercy. **Amen.**

MEDITATION 13

Mary as Mother of the Church and of Our Mission

At the foot of the Cross, Jesus gave us His Mother: *"Behold your mother"* (John 19:27). These were not words for John alone — they were for all of us. In that moment, Mary became the Mother of the Church, the Mother of every believer, the Mother of our mission.

As Mother of the Church, she prays for us, guides us, and nurtures us in the life of grace. As Mother of our mission, she leads us into the heart of her Son's work: the salvation of souls. She does not keep us for herself but sends us out, as she did the servants at Cana, with the command: *"Do whatever He tells you."*

In every age of the Church, Mary has raised up apostles, missionaries, and saints who bring Christ to the world. From the shepherd children of Fatima to the humble Carmelite of Lisieux, she has shown that God chooses the little ones to confound the strong. She wants to do the same with us.

If we allow her to, Mary will form us into true disciples — men and women of prayer, courage, and charity — capable of standing at the foot of the Cross and of carrying it into the world. She will teach us the humility that attracts grace and the boldness that proclaims the Gospel without fear.

Our mission, then, is inseparable from hers: to lead souls to Jesus. Whether in the quiet of a hidden life or the bustle of public ministry, we are called to live as children of Mary, loving Christ as she loves Him, serving others as she serves, and trusting always in God's plan.

Reflection Question:

How is Mary inviting me to participate more fully in the mission of the Church today?

Prayer:

Mary, Mother of the Church, guide my steps, strengthen my faith, and help me to bring Christ to every soul I meet. **Amen.**

Quotes from St. Thérèse of Lisieux and Archbishop Fulton J. Sheen

St. Thérèse of Lisieux Speaks

"She is more Mother than Queen."

"Mary is more a Mother than a Queen, for she loves us and knows our weakness."

"It is the Blessed Virgin who, having lived in obscurity, teaches me how to serve God in the hiddenness of everyday life."

"With Mary, I will stay near the Cross, and with her, I will rise in the joy of Easter."

Archbishop Fulton J. Sheen Speaks

"Mary is not only the Mother of Jesus, but she is the Mother of all those who follow Him. At Bethlehem, she gave birth to the Head; at Calvary, she became the Mother of the Body."

"The closer one comes to Mary, the more one becomes like her Son, for her whole mission is to magnify Him."

"Mary teaches us to stand at the Cross not in bitterness, but in love— seeing even in suffering the shadow of the Resurrection."

"The Mother of Jesus is the quickest, surest, and easiest way to the Heart of her Son."

Scripture Reflections
for the Holy Hour

These passages are offered for prayer and meditation during a Holy Hour of Reparation, especially in union with the Blessed Virgin Mary at the Cross.

Old Testament

Isaiah 7:14

Therefore, the Lord himself will give you a sign. Behold, a young woman shall conceive and bear a son and shall call his name Immanuel.

Isaiah 53:3–5

He was despised and rejected by men; a man of sorrows, and acquainted with grief; and as one from whom men hide their faces he was despised, and we esteemed him not.

Surely he has borne our griefs and carried our sorrows; yet we esteemed him stricken, smitten by God, and afflicted.

But he was wounded for our transgressions, he was bruised for our iniquities; upon him was the chastisement that made us whole, and with his stripes we are healed.

Lamentations 1:12

Is it nothing to you, all you who pass by? Look and see if there is any sorrow like my sorrow which was brought upon me, which the Lord inflicted on the day of his fierce anger.

Zechariah 12:10

And I will pour out on the house of David and the inhabitants of Jerusalem a spirit of compassion and supplication, so that, when they look on him whom they have pierced, they shall mourn for him, as one mourns for an only child, and weep bitterly over him, as one weeps over a first-born.

Gospels

Luke 1:26–38 – The Birth of Jesus Foretold

In the sixth month the angel Gabriel was sent from God to a city of Galilee named Nazareth, to a virgin betrothed to a man whose name was Joseph, of the house of David; and the virgin's name was Mary. And he came to her and said, "Hail, full of grace, the Lord is with you!" But she was greatly troubled at the saying, and considered in her mind what sort of greeting this might be. And the angel said to her, "Do not be afraid, Mary, for you have found favor with God. And behold, you will conceive in your womb and bear a son, and you shall call his name Jesus.

He will be great, and will be called the Son of the Most High; and the Lord God will give to him the throne of his father David, and he will reign over the house of Jacob for ever; and of his kingdom there will be no end."

And Mary said to the angel, "How can this be, since I have no husband?"

And the angel said to her,
"The Holy Spirit will come upon you,
and the power of the Most High will overshadow you;
therefore the child to be born will be called holy,
the Son of God.

And behold, your kinswoman Elizabeth in her old age has also conceived a son; and this is the sixth month with her who was called barren. For with God nothing will be impossible." And Mary said, "Behold, I am the handmaid of the Lord; let it be to me according to your word." And the angel departed from her.

Luke 2:25–35 – The Prophecy of Simeon

Now there was a man in Jerusalem, whose name was Simeon, and this man was righteous and devout, looking for the consolation of Israel, and the Holy Spirit was upon him.

And it had been revealed to him by the Holy Spirit that he should not see death before he had seen the Lord's Christ.

And inspired by the Spirit he came into the temple; and when the parents brought in the child Jesus, to do for him according to the custom of the law, he took him up in his arms and blessed God and said,
Lord, now lettest thou thy servant depart in peace,

according to thy word; for mine eyes have seen thy salvation which thou hast prepared in the presence of all peoples, a light for revelation to the Gentiles, and for glory to thy people Israel."

And his father and his mother marveled at what was said about him; and Simeon blessed them and said to Mary his mother,

"Behold, this child is set for the fall and rising of many in Israel, and for a sign that is spoken against (and a sword will pierce through your own soul also), that thoughts out of many hearts may be revealed."

John 2:1–11 – The Wedding at Cana

On the third day there was a marriage at Cana in Galilee, and the mother of Jesus was there; Jesus also was invited to the marriage, with his disciples. When the wine failed, the mother of Jesus said to him, "They have no wine." And Jesus said to her, "O woman, what have you to do with me? My hour has not yet come." His mother said to the servants, "Do whatever he tells you." Now six stone jars were standing there, for the Jewish rites of purification, each holding twenty or thirty gallons. Jesus said to them, "Fill the jars with water." And they filled them up to the brim. He said to them, "Now draw some out, and take it to the steward of the feast." So they took it. When the steward of the feast tasted the water now become wine, and did not know where it came from (though the servants who had drawn the water knew), the steward of the feast called the bridegroom and said to him, "Every man serves the good wine first; and when men have drunk freely, then the poor wine; but you have kept the good wine until now." This, the first of his signs, Jesus did at Cana in Galilee, and manifested his glory; and his disciples believed in him.

John 19:25–27 – Mary at the Foot of the Cross

So the soldiers did this. But standing by the cross of Jesus were his mother, and his mother's sister, Mary the wife of Clopas, and Mary Magdalene. When Jesus saw his mother, and the disciple whom he loved standing near, he said to his mother, "Woman, behold, your son!" Then he said to the disciple, "Behold, your mother!" And from that hour the disciple took her to his own home.

Acts & Epistles

Acts 1:14

All these with one accord devoted themselves to prayer, together with the women and Mary the mother of Jesus, and with his brethren.

Galatians 4:4–5

But when the time had fully come, God sent forth his Son, born of woman, born under the law, to redeem those who were under the law, so that we might receive adoption as sons.

Hebrews 12:1–3 - The Example of Jesus

Therefore, since we are surrounded by so great a cloud of witnesses, let us also lay aside every weight, and sin which clings so closely, and let us run with perseverance the race that is set before us, looking to Jesus the pioneer and perfecter of our faith, who for the joy that was set before him endured the cross, despising the shame, and is seated at the right hand of the throne of God. Consider him who endured from sinners such hostility against himself, so that you may not grow weary or fainthearted.

Fulton Sheen's
Holy Hour Reflections

1. Why Make a Holy Hour with Mary?

There are as many reasons for making a Holy Hour as there are souls who love Jesus. The essential reason is this: **love seeks company.** When you love someone, you wish to be near them—not only to speak, but to listen, to gaze, to be silent together.

The Blessed Mother understood this perfectly. She spent thirty years in the hidden life with her Son, treasuring every word and every gesture in her Immaculate Heart (Luke 2:19). At Calvary, she kept her place beside Him even when the world turned away. Your Holy Hour is a continuation of that Marian faithfulness—standing spiritually beside the Cross.

Our Lord asked, *"Could you not watch one hour with Me?"* (Matthew 26:40). Mary answered that call with her whole life. To make a Holy Hour is to join her in consoling the Heart of Christ—adoring Him, loving Him, and offering reparation for the coldness and ingratitude He still receives.

Fulton Sheen wrote:

> *"The purpose of the Holy Hour is to encourage a deep personal encounter with Christ. It is not an hour of lecturing, but of loving; not of talking, but of listening; not of reading, but of adoring."*

When your Holy Hour is made *with Mary*, she teaches you how to listen deeply. She whispers in your heart the words she once said at Cana: *"Do whatever He tells you"* (John 2:5).

In the world's eyes, an hour spent in quiet adoration may seem unproductive. But in Heaven's view, that hour — offered with Mary — is rich beyond measure. Sheen often said that the world is not dying from lack of work, but from lack of prayer. If more souls would unite themselves to Christ in the Eucharist with Mary, there would be more strength for the Church, more holiness among priests, more conversions among sinners, and more peace in the world.

The Holy Hour is also a powerful **act of reparation**. The Immaculate Heart of Mary still suffers because her Son is wounded by indifference and sin. When you kneel in adoration and pray with her, you are helping to console both Hearts — offering love where there has been coldness, fidelity where there has been betrayal, and hope where there has been despair.

> *"To watch one hour with Jesus, in the company of Mary, is to repair a thousand hours of the world's forgetfulness."*

2. How to Make a Holy Hour with Mary

There is no single formula for making a Holy Hour, but the saints teach us that certain dispositions open the soul most fully to grace. When you make a Holy Hour **with Mary**, it becomes not only your prayer, but *hers* — and she presents it, adorned with her purity and love, to her Son.

Begin with Presence

Enter the church or chapel with a Marian heart. Remember how Mary approached her Son at Cana — with confidence, reverence, and love. Genuflect slowly, consciously, as if you were greeting Him in person — because you are.

Sheen often encouraged beginning the hour by **offering it in reparation** — for your own sins, for those of your family, for priests, and for the whole Church. Mary's Immaculate Heart will join your intention to hers, making it pleasing to the Sacred Heart of Jesus.

> *"Through Mary, we go to Jesus more quickly, more gently, and more perfectly."*
>
> **— St. Louis de Montfort**

A Suggested Structure

You may divide the hour into three parts — though Mary may inspire you to linger in one part longer than another:

1) **Adoration and Love** – Simply gaze upon the Eucharistic Face of Jesus. You may pray silently:

   "Lord Jesus, I am here with Your Mother. Look upon me as You looked upon her at Calvary." Let Mary help you adore, just as she adored Him in Bethlehem, in Nazareth, and at the Cross.

2) **Reparation and Intercession** – Speak to Him of the wounds of His Church and of the world. Offer your own heart, united with Mary's, to repair for sin. Use prayers like the **Chaplet of the Holy Face** or the **Seven Sorrows of Mary**.

3) **Listening and Union** – Be still. Allow His words to echo in your heart, as they did in Mary's. She will teach you to ponder, to treasure, and to surrender.

Scripture with Mary

Reading the Gospels during a Holy Hour can be especially fruitful when seen through Mary's eyes. For example:

I. At the **Annunciation** (Luke 1:26–38), contemplate her "yes" and ask for the grace to say your own.

II. At the **Visitation** (Luke 1:39–56), join her in bringing Christ's presence to others.

III. At the **Cross** (John 19:25–27), receive her anew as your Mother.

End with Thanksgiving

Before leaving, thank Jesus for the gift of this hour and thank Mary for leading you into His presence. Sheen advised making a simple resolution to carry a grace from the hour into your daily life — perhaps more patience, more charity, or a deeper devotion to Our Lady.

Leave quietly, carrying in your soul the peace Mary always leaves behind.

> *"A Holy Hour in the presence of the Eucharist is worth more than a thousand sermons."*
>
> — **Fulton J. Sheen.**

When made with Mary, it becomes even more — a rehearsal for eternity, when we will adore Him forever with her.

How to Begin Your Own Holy Hour of Reparation

A Holy Hour of Reparation is more than a devotional practice — it is an intimate encounter with the Heart of Jesus through the Heart of Mary. In *Behold Your Mother*, we are invited to make this hour in union with Our Blessed Mother, who stood faithfully at the foot of the Cross.

Just as St. John welcomed Mary into his home (John 19:27), we welcome her into our prayer. She becomes our model and companion in making reparation to the Sacred Heart of Jesus, especially for the sins and indifference committed against Him.

1. Preparing for the Hour

I.   **Choose the time and place.** Ideally, make your Holy Hour before the Blessed Sacrament, exposed or reserved in the tabernacle. If this is not possible, set aside a quiet space in your home with a crucifix and an image of Our Lady.

II. **Bring your spiritual aids.** A Rosary, Holy Scriptures, a prayer book, and any Marian devotions (such as the Seven Sorrows or the Litany of Loreto).

III. **Unite your intention with Mary's.** Begin by asking the Blessed Mother to lend you her heart so that you may love Jesus with her purity, faith, and unwavering fidelity.

2. Structure of the Hour

While the Holy Spirit may guide you differently from time to time, the following structure can help:

a) *Opening Act of Consecration*

Offer yourself entirely to Jesus through Mary, acknowledging her as the perfect guide in reparation and intercession.

b) *Scripture and Meditation*

Read a passage that draws you into the mystery of Mary at the Cross—such as John 19:25-27 or Luke 2:34-35. Meditate on how her Immaculate Heart suffered in union with her Son.

c) *Prayer of Reparation*

Offer prayers specifically in atonement for sins against the Sacred Heart of Jesus and the Immaculate Heart of Mary—blasphemies, neglect, sacrilege, and indifference.

d) *Marian Devotion*

Pray the Rosary or the Seven Sorrows in a spirit of reparation, uniting each mystery to Mary's participation in Christ's saving work.

e) *Silent Adoration*

Spend a few moments simply gazing at Jesus — through the eyes of Mary. Ask her to help you listen to His voice and console His Heart.

f) Closing Act of Praise and Thanksgiving

Thank Jesus and Mary for the grace of this hour. Offer it for the Church, for priests, for sinners, and for the triumph of the Immaculate Heart.

3. Perseverance in the Practice

1) **Choose a regular time.** Whether weekly or daily, faithfulness deepens the grace of reparation.

2) **Invite Mary into each Hour.** Begin every Holy Hour by placing yourself in her hands, asking her to shape your prayer as she shaped her own at Calvary.

3) **Offer your trials as prayer.** Unite your sufferings — great or small — to the Cross, placing them into Mary's hands as a bouquet for Jesus.

> *"To Jesus through Mary — there is no surer path, no more perfect way to console His Heart."*

CONCLUDING WORD

Sent from the Foot of the Cross

From Calvary resounds the command of Christ: "Behold your mother." This is no suggestion, but a gift and a mission. To behold Mary is to welcome her into the intimacy of our homes, our prayer, our very hearts. She is Mother of the Church, Mother of priests, Mother of souls longing for holiness. Fulton Sheen reminds us that whenever we draw close to Mary, she points us unerringly to her Son.

As these reflections end, let them begin anew in your life. Entrust your crosses to Mary's hands; consecrate your joys to her Immaculate Heart. With her, the darkest nights become dawn, and every suffering can be united to the redeeming love of Jesus. May our last word echo the first command: *Behold your Mother.*

THE CROSS
AND THE
LAST WORDS

INRI

Meditations on Calvary and the Interior Life

A SHEEN MISSION SERIES • VOLUME III

THE CROSS AND
THE LAST WORDS

Meditations with Fulton J. Sheen
on Calvary and the Interior Life
A Sheen Mission Series – Volume III

The Sheen Mission Series invites you to walk with Archbishop Fulton J. Sheen in prayer, reparation, and renewal — a journey of the Holy Face, the Cross, the Eucharist, and Our Blessed Mother.

Description:

*T*he *Cross and the Last Words* is the third volume in the Sheen Mission Series — a treasury of meditations on Calvary and the Seven Last Words of Christ.

Archbishop Fulton Sheen, known worldwide for his preaching on the Cross, offers profound insights into forgiveness, mercy, suffering, and hope. This volume invites you to stand at the foot of the Cross, to hear again the words of the dying Christ, and to discover their power to heal and renew your life.

> *"Calvary is the mountain where all the love of God is revealed. In the Seven Last Words, we hear the heart of Christ speaking to the heart of the world."*

> **— Archbishop Fulton J. Sheen**

EPIGRAPH

"When they came to the place which is called The Skull, there they crucified him, and the criminals, one on the right and one on the left. And Jesus said, 'Father, forgive them; for they know not what they do.' ... Then Jesus, crying with a loud voice, said, 'Father, into thy hands I commit my spirit!' And having said this he breathed his last."

— Luke 23:33–46

"The Cross is not merely an incident in the life of Our Lord; it is the mission pulpit from which He preaches to the world His most eloquent sermon — the sermon of redeeming love."

—Archbishop Fulton J. Sheen
(The Seven Last Words)

FOREWORD

The Cross is the pulpit from which Christ preached His greatest sermon. Each word spoken from Calvary was not only addressed to those gathered beneath the wood, but to every soul across time who would dare to listen.

Archbishop Fulton J. Sheen made it his life's mission to help the world listen again. For fifty-eight consecutive Good Fridays, he offered meditations on the Seven Last Words of Jesus. His voice echoed across cathedrals, airwaves, and television screens, reminding the faithful that these words are not relics of the past but living streams of mercy for the present.

Why do we return to the Cross? Because in a world wounded by sin, suffering, and division, the last words of Christ reveal a medicine stronger than our wounds. They unveil the depth of divine love, the gravity of human sin, and the triumph of mercy over despair.

This book is not simply a collection of meditations; it is a pilgrimage. Each reflection invites you to kneel at the foot of Calvary, to hear anew the words of the dying Christ, and to let them heal and renew your heart.

Archbishop Sheen often said, "Unless there is a Good Friday in your life, there can be no Easter Sunday." May these pages help you embrace the Cross, not as a symbol of sorrow alone, but as the surest path to resurrection.

INTRODUCTION

Why the Cross? Why Now?

E very age has its question, its trial, its wound. For our time, it is the flight from suffering. We run from the Cross in search of comfort, distraction, or control — and yet in doing so, we run from the very place where love is revealed.

Why the Cross? Because it is here that human sin and divine mercy meet. It is here that the ugliness of hatred is overcome by the beauty of sacrifice. It is here that we see, not in theory but in flesh and blood, what love truly means. The Cross is not an accessory to Christianity; it is its center. Without it, our faith becomes sentiment. With it, our faith becomes salvation.

Archbishop Fulton J. Sheen once said, *"The Cross is the only ladder high enough to touch Heaven."* To gaze upon it is to discover the measure of God's love and the seriousness of our sin. To embrace it is to find not defeat but redemption, not sorrow but joy, not death but life.

Why now? Because the world has never been more in need of meaning. We suffer — in body, in mind, in spirit — and yet so often without purpose. The Cross gives purpose. It tells us that pain is not wasted, that wounds can be healed, and that sacrifice can redeem. It transforms tragedy into triumph and sorrow into song.

Archbishop Fulton Sheen once observed that Calvary is the place where the drama of human sin and divine mercy meet. It is here that we discover the meaning of our own trials, for the Cross is not simply the story of what Christ endured — it is the key to what we are called to become.

In an age that seeks to escape suffering, Christ invites us to enter it with Him. He does not promise a life without crosses; He promises that no cross will be without Him. And in that promise, we find hope.

This volume is an invitation to stand with Mary, with John, and with the repentant thief — to hear again the words of Jesus from the Cross and to let them shape our hearts. Each meditation is a call to reparation, to surrender, to trust. Each word is a gift.

Let us then take up the ancient prayer of the Church: *"We adore You, O Christ, and we bless You, because by Your Holy Cross You have redeemed the world."*

MEDITATION 1

The Cross and the
Mystery of Suffering

Reflection – The Core Lesson of Suffering

Suffering is not an elective in the school of life — it is a required course. For some, it arrives like a sudden storm; for others, it lingers like a long shadow. Our first instinct is often escape. But the Cross teaches us to ask a different question: *Who suffers with me?*

Archbishop Fulton Sheen reminded us that Calvary is the only classroom where pain finds meaning. "When we suffer without Christ," he said, "we suffer alone; when we suffer with Christ, we share in the work of redemption."

Sheen on Redemptive Suffering

"In the modern world, there is much concern for eliminating suffering, but little understanding of its place in the plan of God. Our Lord did not come to remove the Cross from life, but to lift life into the Cross, making it redemptive. By uniting our wounds to His, we discover that pain can be fruitful, love can be purified, and hope can be born from ashes."

Sheen saw suffering not as an interruption to God's plan but as an instrument of it. The nails did not hold Christ to the Cross — love did. And that same love can hold us steady when our own trials press hard.

Illustration – A Mother's Loss

There is the story of a mother who, after losing her child, chose to offer her grief to parents who had never known faith. She could not undo her loss, but she could decide what her loss would mean. Like the Blessed Mother at Calvary, she stood in the place where pain and faith meet — and chose to believe that the Cross is never the end.

Her witness became light to others in darkness. Through her tears, she revealed the same truth the Cross reveals: suffering, when united to Christ, becomes a channel of mercy.

Invitation – Choosing the Meaning of Our Cross

If suffering is inevitable, we must decide whether it will be wasted or offered. Christ's Cross teaches us to "waste nothing" — not a tear, not a sleepless night, not a hidden wound. Every trial can become a prayer, every sorrow a seed of compassion.

Stand at Calvary with Mary and John. Look upon the Crucified and ask:

- *What Cross am I carrying right now?*

- *Am I carrying it alone, or with Him?*

When we surrender our suffering to the Cross, it ceases to be only ours. It becomes His — and in Him, it becomes redemptive.

Closing Prayer

Lord Jesus, You carried the weight of the world's sin upon Your shoulders. Teach me to unite my sorrows to Yours, so that nothing in my life may be wasted. May every wound become a window for Your grace, every trial an offering of love. Keep me at the foot of Your Cross, where suffering is no longer meaningless but fruitful in Your mercy. **Amen.**

MEDITATION 2

The Cross as the School of Love

Reflection – Learning Love at Calvary

Every human heart longs to love and be loved, yet our understanding of love is often shallow. We mistake it for sentiment, possession, or passing desire. The Cross reveals something different: love that is sacrificial, steadfast, and willing to suffer for the beloved.

On Calvary, Jesus does not merely speak of love — He demonstrates it. His arms, stretched wide upon the wood, become the open classroom where we learn that true love always costs something.

Sheen on Love's Lesson

> *"Love is not measured by how much it receives, but by how much it gives. The Cross is not only the proof of Christ's love for us; it is the pattern of what our love must be for others. Love that refuses sacrifice is not love at all."*

Archbishop Sheen insisted that Calvary is the "school of love," where every disciple must sit and learn. In a world that prizes comfort and convenience, the Cross teaches that love is forged in fire, not in ease.

Illustration – A Hidden Sacrifice

A priest once shared the story of an elderly parishioner who, after years of caring for her disabled husband, whispered: *"I thought I was keeping him alive, but he was teaching me how to love."*

Her daily acts — spoon-feeding, lifting, bathing, praying beside his bed — were hidden from the world, but radiant before God. Like Mary at the foot of the Cross, she discovered that love is not defined by ease but by endurance.

Invitation – Enrolling in Love's School

The Cross is not an optional course in the Christian life; it is the very curriculum. Every wound we bear, every burden we carry, becomes a lesson in love when united to Christ.

Ask yourself:

- *Where am I being invited to love beyond comfort?*

- *Who in my life needs not just my affection, but my sacrifice?*

- *Am I willing to let the Cross teach me love — even when it hurts?*

To sit at the foot of the Cross is to let Jesus Himself tutor us in the ways of self-giving.

Closing Prayer

Crucified Lord, Teacher of Love, show me that true love is more than words — it is sacrifice. Give me patience when I grow weary, generosity when I want to withdraw, and courage when love demands a Cross. May Your school of Calvary shape my heart, until it beats in union with Yours. **Amen.**

MEDITATION 3

The First Word
"Father, Forgive Them"

Reflection – The Scandal of Forgiveness

The first word from the Cross is not a cry of protest, but a prayer of mercy. In the face of betrayal, injustice, and cruelty, Jesus does not condemn His executioners. He asks the Father to forgive them.

This moment unveils the heart of God: mercy poured out where vengeance might have been expected. At Calvary, forgiveness is no longer an idea — it becomes flesh and blood.

Sheen on Mercy at the Cross

"The world expected anger, but Christ gave pardon. The Cross is not only the pulpit of pain, it is the pulpit of forgiveness. If we are to be His disciples, then we must forgive — not seven times, but seventy times seven."

Archbishop Sheen taught that Christ's first word shatters the cycle of hatred. He reveals that evil is not overcome by more evil, but by love that refuses retaliation.

Illustration – A Prisoner's Conversion

A chaplain once recounted the story of a man imprisoned for violence, whose heart was hardened by years of bitterness. One day, reading the words of Jesus on the Cross — *"Father, forgive them"* — he realized he had never forgiven those who had hurt him, nor sought forgiveness for his own crimes.

That encounter became the turning point of his life. He began to pray daily for his victims and for the grace to forgive. Slowly, the chains around his soul were loosed. Mercy set him free long before the prison gates ever would.

Invitation – Living the First Word

The hardest words to say are often the simplest: *"I forgive you."* Yet without them, peace remains impossible. The Cross shows us that forgiveness is not weakness but strength — the strength to love as God loves.

Ask yourself:

- *Who do I still hold in the prison of my resentment?*

- *Where is Christ inviting me to break the cycle of anger?*

- *Am I willing to pray, even through tears, "Father, forgive them" for those who have wounded me?*

Closing Prayer

Merciful Jesus, Your first word from the Cross was forgiveness. Teach me to forgive as You forgive — freely, fully, and without condition. Heal the wounds in my heart that resist mercy. Let my life echo Your prayer, until every bitterness is consumed in Your love. **Amen.**

MEDITATION 4

The Second Word: "This Day You Will Be with Me in Paradise"

Reflection – The Promise of Mercy

Beside Christ hung two criminals. One cursed, the other confessed. One turned inward in despair, the other outward in hope. To the repentant thief, Jesus spoke a word more precious than freedom: "This day you will be with Me in Paradise."

This second word reveals the immediacy of grace. Heaven is not a reward for the perfect, but a gift for the repentant. In a single act of trust — *"Jesus, remember me"* — a sinner gained eternity.

Sheen on the Good Thief

> *"The thief on the right had no good works to his credit, no reputation to uphold, no promises he could keep. He had only a heart that could trust. And that was enough. In one instant, a lifetime of sin was swallowed up by a moment of faith."*

Archbishop Sheen loved to point out that the thief stole heaven in the final hour. He is the patron saint of hope for every soul who fears it is too late.

Illustration – A Deathbed Grace

A priest once recalled being called to the bedside of a man who had not entered a church in over fifty years. With tears, the man whispered: *"Father, is it too late for me?"* The priest placed the crucifix in his hands and repeated the words of Christ to the thief: *"This day you will be with Me in Paradise."*

That dying man, like the good thief, found peace in surrender. His last breath was not a sigh of despair, but of hope — proof that God's mercy never comes too late.

Invitation – Trusting the Promise

The thief's prayer is short, simple, and unforgettable: *"Jesus, remember me."* It is a prayer anyone can pray, in joy or sorrow, in strength or weakness. It is the prayer of a child returning home.

Ask yourself:

- *Do I believe God's mercy can reach even the darkest corners of my life?*

- *Am I willing to entrust my future — and my eternity — to His promise?*

- *Who in my life needs to hear the hope that it is never too late to turn back to God?*

Closing Prayer

Jesus, Savior of the lost, remember me when my strength fails and my heart falters. Remember me in my weakness, and bring me into the light of Your Kingdom. Let my last words echo the prayer of the good thief: "Jesus, remember me." **Amen.**

MEDITATION 5

The Third Word
"Behold Your Mother"

Reflection – A Gift from the Cross

At Calvary, Jesus looked down and saw His Mother and the beloved disciple. With His strength waning, He entrusted them to each other: *"Woman, behold your son ... Behold your mother."*

This third word is not only about Mary and John. It is about us. In His final moments, Christ gave His Mother to every believer. At the foot of the Cross, we received not only forgiveness but family.

Sheen on Mary's Mission

> *"Mary is not just a memory in the drama of Calvary. She is the Mother whom Christ gave to us that we might never again be orphans. At the foot of the Cross, she became the Mother of all who would be reborn in grace."*

Archbishop Sheen taught that Christ, by giving us His Mother, gave us the perfect companion for the journey of faith. She consoles, intercedes, and teaches us how to remain at the Cross when others flee.

Illustration – A Soldier's Consolation

A young soldier, gravely wounded, was once asked in his last hours what brought him peace. He pointed to a medal of the Blessed Virgin around his neck and whispered: *"She is my Mother. I am not afraid."*

Like John, he discovered that in Mary's presence, we are never alone. Her maternal love draws us closer to Jesus and strengthens us to endure our own crosses.

Invitation – Receiving Our Mother

Jesus' gift of Mary is not symbolic. It is real, personal, and enduring. Each of us is invited to take her into our homes, into our hearts, and into our daily prayer.

Ask yourself:

- *Have I truly welcomed Mary as my Mother, or kept her at a distance?*

- *Do I bring my struggles to her, as a child brings them to a parent?*

- *How can I imitate John by making space for her in my life today?*

Closing Prayer

Mary, Mother of Jesus and my Mother, teach me to stand faithfully at the Cross. Comfort me in sorrow, strengthen me in trial, and lead me always to your Son. May I never forget that you are near, and that in your embrace I am never alone. **Amen.**

MEDITATION 6

The Fourth Word: "My God, My God, Why Have You Forsaken Me?"

Reflection – The Cry of Abandonment

At the height of His agony, Jesus cried out the words of Psalm 22: *"My God, my God, why have You forsaken Me?"* This is perhaps the most haunting of the Seven Last Words. It reveals not only the depth of His suffering but also the depth of His love — for He chose to enter even into the experience of seeming abandonment.

This cry is not despair, but prayer. In uttering the Psalm, Jesus shows us that even in the darkest night, the soul can cling to God.

Sheen on the Mystery of Forsakenness

> *"There is no suffering in the world which He did not make His own. In crying out to the Father, He gave a voice to every lonely soul, every broken heart, every abandoned child. He was not forsaken so that we might never be."*

Archbishop Sheen explained that Christ bore the silence of God so that we would never have to face it alone. What seems to be absence is, in truth, the most profound nearness.

Illustration – A Silent Night of Faith

A religious sister once endured years of spiritual dryness, feeling that God had hidden His face from her. She later confided: *"In that silence, I learned to love Him without consolation. I discovered that faith is not about feelings but about fidelity."*

Her hidden trial reflected the mystery of Christ's cry — that love endures even when heaven seems silent.

Invitation – Praying Through the Silence

Every Christian, at some point, feels the shadow of abandonment: unanswered prayers, losses, loneliness. Christ has already stood there, sanctifying that place with His presence.

Ask yourself:

- *When have I felt abandoned by God?*

- *Can I unite that pain with Christ's cry on the Cross?*

- *Am I willing to keep praying, even when God seems silent?*

Closing Prayer

Jesus, who cried to the Father in the hour of darkness, be with me when I feel forsaken. Teach me to trust that even in silence, the Father's love is near. May my own cry of pain become a prayer of faith, until it is answered in the light of Your Resurrection. **Amen.**

MEDITATION 7

The Fifth Word: "I Thirst"

Reflection – The Cry of Desire

After hours of agony, Jesus spoke two simple words: *"I thirst."* On one level, it was the physical thirst of a body drained of blood and strength. But beneath it lies a deeper truth: the thirst of God for souls.

The Cross reveals that Christ's longing is not for water alone, but for love — your love, my love, the love of every human heart. His thirst is the eternal desire that none be lost.

Sheen on the Thirst of Christ

> *"When He said, 'I thirst,' He was not only asking for water. He was thirsting for souls, thirsting for our love, thirsting for the return of the creatures He came to redeem. His thirst still remains — for until the last soul is saved, His Heart is not satisfied."*

Archbishop Sheen reminded us that the thirst of Christ is ongoing. He thirsts not only from the Cross, but in every tabernacle, every altar, every soul that still wanders far from Him.

Illustration – The Missionary's Encounter

A missionary once shared how he preached about Christ's thirst in a remote village. A young woman approached afterward and said: *"I never knew God desired me. I thought I was the one chasing Him. Now I see that He has been thirsting for me all along."*

Her discovery changed her life. She entered the Church, not out of fear, but out of the joy of being wanted by God.

Invitation – Quenching His Thirst

Jesus' cry is a call to each of us. He thirsts for our faith, our love, our surrender. And He thirsts through the needs of others — the poor, the lonely, the forgotten. To love them is to give Him drink.

Ask yourself:

- *Do I believe that Jesus truly thirsts for me personally?*

- *How can I offer Him the drink of my love today?*

- *Where is He thirsting in the suffering of others around me?*

Closing Prayer

O Jesus, burning with thirst upon the Cross, quench Your longing in my poor love. Take my heart as Your refreshment, my prayers as Your drink, my acts of charity as Your consolation. May I never forget that You thirst for me, and may I thirst only for You. **Amen.**

MEDITATION 8

The Sixth Word: "It Is Finished"

Reflection – The Triumph of Completion

As His final moments approached, Jesus proclaimed: *"It is finished."* These words are not a sigh of defeat but a declaration of victory. The work the Father had given Him — the work of redemption — was now complete.

The Cross reveals that love does not stop halfway. Christ embraced every suffering, every humiliation, every drop of the chalice of sacrifice. Nothing was left undone.

Sheen on the Fulfillment of the Cross

> *"When Our Lord said, 'It is finished,' He was not saying, 'It is over.' He was saying, 'It is accomplished.' The world's salvation was won, the debt was paid, the sacrifice complete. No task was left unfulfilled, no suffering wasted."*

Archbishop Sheen taught that these words remind us that true love perseveres to the end. Our vocations, our duties, our crosses are not measured by beginnings alone, but by fidelity to completion.

Illustration – A Life Faithfully Lived

A nun who had served in hidden poverty for fifty years was once asked what gave her strength. She answered simply: *"I just wanted to finish what God gave me to do."*

Her life bore no fame, no worldly reward. Yet in her quiet perseverance, she mirrored the words of Christ: *"It is finished."* Love had been carried through to the end.

Invitation – Persevering in Love

The sixth word invites us to reflect on our own commitments — to God, to family, to vocation. Do we carry them only when easy, or do we persevere to completion?

Ask yourself:

- *What mission or duty has God entrusted to me that I am tempted to leave unfinished?*

- *Can I offer my daily sacrifices as part of Christ's completed work of love?*

- *Am I willing to remain faithful to the end, trusting that nothing offered in love is wasted?*

Closing Prayer

Lord Jesus, who finished the work the Father gave You, strengthen me to persevere in the tasks entrusted to me. When I grow weary, remind me of Your Cross. When I am tempted to quit, remind me of Your love. Let me one day echo Your words with peace: "It is finished." **Amen.**

MEDITATION 9

The Seventh Word: "Father, Into Your Hands I Commit My Spirit"

Reflection – The Surrender of the Son

The final word of Jesus is a prayer of trust: *"Father, into Your hands I commit My spirit."* After the agony, after the darkness, after the silence, He rests everything in the Father's embrace.

This is the summit of the Cross — surrender. The One who came from the Father now returns to Him, teaching us that the end of every life, if lived in faith, is not despair but homecoming.

Sheen on the Peace of Surrender

> *"Our Lord died as He lived: offering Himself in perfect obedience to the Father. The Cross was not taken from Him; it was freely given. In surrendering His spirit, He shows us that the last act of life is not to cling, but to commend."*

Archbishop Sheen reminded us that death, in Christ, is no longer the great terror. It has become the final act of love — a placing of our lives back into the Father's hands.

Illustration – A Childlike Trust

A saintly priest was once asked what he feared most about dying. He replied: *"Nothing. For I know whose hands will catch me when I fall."*

His answer reflects the heart of Christ's final word: trust as simple and complete as that of a child leaping into a father's arms.

Invitation – Learning to Let Go

Every day offers opportunities to practice this surrender: letting go of control, of fear, of our own will. In small deaths — of pride, of resentment, of selfishness — we prepare for that final surrender into the Father's hands.

Ask yourself:

- *What am I still clinging to that I need to entrust to God?*

- *Can I make of my life a daily act of surrender, echoing Jesus' final word?*

- *Do I live with the confidence that my true home is with the Father?*

Closing Prayer

Father, into Your hands I commend my spirit. Take what I fear to surrender, hold what I cannot carry, and receive what I cannot keep. At the hour of my death, may I rest in Your embrace, with the peace of Christ upon my lips. **Amen.**

MEDITATION 10

Calvary in Daily Life

Reflection – The Cross Beyond Good Friday

Calvary is not only a hill outside Jerusalem; it is the pattern of every Christian life. Each day offers a share in Christ's sacrifice — in small annoyances, hidden sacrifices, quiet sufferings, and moments of fidelity.

To live the Christian life is to carry the Cross not only in church, but at home, at work, in family struggles, in disappointments, and even in the silence of unanswered prayers. Calvary continues wherever love meets suffering.

Sheen on Everyday Crosses

> *"There is no escaping the Cross. We can either drag it, cursing the weight, or we can embrace it, finding in it the seed of redemption. The difference is not in the Cross itself, but in the spirit with which we carry it."*

Archbishop Sheen insisted that our daily trials, united with Christ, become channels of grace. When borne with love, even the smallest crosses can sanctify the soul and bless the world.

Illustration – The Hidden Heroism of the Ordinary

A father rises early to provide for his family, enduring long hours with patience. A mother silently offers her exhaustion in caring for her children. A sick parishioner unites his suffering to the Lord for the salvation of souls.

None of these acts will be recorded in history books, but in heaven, they shine brighter than gold. They are Calvary lived in ordinary life.

Invitation – Embracing Daily Crosses

Each day we face a choice: to resent our burdens or to offer them. In the school of the Cross, nothing is wasted when placed in Christ's hands.

Ask yourself:

- *What small cross can I carry with love today?*

- *Do I see the hidden sufferings of my life as obstacles, or as opportunities for grace?*

- *Am I willing to let my daily life become a continuation of Calvary?*

Closing Prayer

Lord Jesus, teach me to find Calvary in the ordinary moments of my life. Help me embrace my daily crosses, not with bitterness, but with love. May every sacrifice, however small, be joined to Yours, until my whole life becomes an offering upon the altar of Your Cross. **Amen.**

MEDITATION 11

Healing at the Foot of the Cross

Reflection – Where Wounds Meet Mercy

At the foot of the Cross, the broken find their healing. Mary, John, and the faithful few stood near Jesus as His blood and water flowed forth — streams of mercy for the wounded world.

The Cross is not only a place of suffering but also a fountain of grace. To kneel at Calvary is to discover that our wounds are not the end; they can become the place where God's mercy enters.

Sheen on the Cross as Medicine

> *"The Cross is the hospital of souls. It is there we learn that our sickness is sin, and our remedy is grace. No wound is too deep, no scar too lasting, that it cannot be healed by the pierced Heart of Christ."*

Archbishop Sheen often spoke of the Cross as both diagnosis and cure — it reveals the gravity of sin, but also the greater power of redemption.

Illustration – A Pilgrim's Peace

A pilgrim once entered a chapel of the Crucifixion, carrying years of resentment and guilt. As she gazed at the crucified Lord, her tears fell like rain. Later she testified: *"For the first time, I felt forgiven. My wounds were still there, but they were no longer poisoned. They were touched by His wounds."*

Her experience reflects what countless souls discover: healing begins not by running from the Cross but by standing beneath it.

Invitation – Bringing Our Wounds to the Cross

Every heart carries scars: from sin, betrayal, illness, or loss. Calvary invites us to place those wounds into the wounded hands of Christ. Only there do they become transformed.

Ask yourself:

- *What wound in my life most needs the healing touch of Christ?*

- *Am I willing to let His mercy flow into that pain, even if it means reopening it in prayer?*

- *How can I be a source of healing for others by leading them to the Cross?*

Closing Prayer

Jesus, Divine Physician, I bring You the wounds of my heart. Touch them with Your pierced hands, cleanse them with the water and blood from Your side, and make of them channels of compassion for others. At the foot of Your Cross, may I find not despair but healing, not death but new life. **Amen.**

MEDITATION 12

Living in the Shadow of the Cross

Reflection – The Cross as Our Daily Companion

The Cross is not only an event of the past; it casts its shadow across every age and every soul. To live in its shadow is not to live in despair, but to live in the constant reminder of God's love poured out for us.

The shadow of the Cross follows us in our trials, in our choices, and in our prayer. It reminds us that there is no suffering Christ has not shared, no darkness He has not entered, and no burden He will not help us carry.

Sheen on the Ever-Present Cross

> *"Calvary is not just a place; it is a condition. We do not escape the Cross by avoiding it, but by carrying it with Christ. The Christian never leaves Calvary — he carries its shadow with him wherever he goes."*

Archbishop Sheen explained that the Cross is the Christian's constant companion. It teaches us how to live, how to love, and even how to die — always in union with the One who bore it first.

Illustration – A Hidden Witness

A layman once testified that for years he kept a small crucifix in his pocket. Whenever he felt tempted, discouraged, or lonely, he would hold it tightly and whisper: *"I am not alone. He is with me."*

That simple practice became his way of living in the shadow of the Cross — not as a burden, but as a source of strength.

Invitation – Embracing the Shadow

To live in the shadow of the Cross is to let every part of our life be touched by Calvary. Our joys and sorrows, our work and rest, our prayers and relationships — all can be sanctified when brought beneath its shadow.

Ask yourself:

- *Do I see the Cross as something far away, or as a daily presence in my life?*

- *How can I let the remembrance of the Cross shape my choices today?*

- *Am I willing to let its shadow fall on my life, not as darkness, but as light?*

Closing Prayer

Lord Jesus, keep me always in the shadow of Your Cross. When I am tempted, remind me of Your victory. When I am weary, remind me of Your love. When I am joyful, remind me of Your sacrifice. May every step I take be illumined by the shadow that saves. **Amen.**

MEDITATION 13

The Power of the Resurrection through the Cross

Reflection – The Light Beyond the Darkness

The Cross and the Resurrection are inseparable. Calvary was not the end; it was the doorway to Easter morning. By embracing the Cross, Jesus transformed it into the very path of glory.

For the Christian, this means that every suffering united with Christ carries within it a seed of resurrection. Death is not the final word. Love is.

Sheen on the Triumph of the Cross

> *"The world thinks of the Cross as failure. But without Good Friday, there would be no Easter. Christ has turned the Cross from a symbol of defeat into the very condition of victory. In every Christian life, the Cross is the prelude to resurrection."*

Archbishop Sheen taught that the Resurrection does not cancel the Cross, but crowns it. The wounds remain, but they shine with glory.

Illustration – Hope after Loss

A widow once reflected that after her husband's death, she felt buried in grief. But slowly, as she united her sorrow to Christ, she began to see signs of new life: deeper prayer, compassion for others, and an unshakable hope in eternal reunion.

Her testimony echoed Easter morning — the dawn that rises only after the long night of Good Friday.

Invitation – Living the Paschal Mystery

Every trial we endure can become a share in the Paschal Mystery — Cross and Resurrection. To embrace the Cross is to trust that new life will follow, though unseen for now.

Ask yourself:

- *Where do I need to believe that God can bring resurrection from my suffering?*

- *Do I live with the hope that no cross is final?*

- *Am I willing to let Christ's victory be my confidence, even in dark hours?*

Closing Prayer

Risen Lord, You turned the Cross into victory and death into life. Teach me to see my trials as seeds of resurrection. Fill me with hope that no suffering is wasted, and that Easter always follows Good Friday. May I live in the joy of Your triumph, and share it with all I meet. **Amen.**

MEDITATION 14

The Cross and the Eucharist

Reflection – Calvary Made Present

At the Last Supper, Jesus gave His disciples bread and wine, saying: *"This is My Body ... This is My Blood."* On Calvary, He fulfilled that gift with His sacrifice. The Eucharist is not a memory of the Cross but its living presence.

Every Mass is Calvary renewed — the same Body broken, the same Blood poured out, offered now for us in sacramental form. To approach the Eucharist is to stand at the foot of the Cross and receive its grace.

Sheen on the Eucharistic Sacrifice

> *"The Mass is the re-presentation of Calvary. The difference is that on Calvary Christ was alone; in the Mass, He invites us to join Him. The Cross is lifted out of history and made present on every altar of the world."*

Archbishop Sheen emphasized that the Eucharist is the continuation of the Cross. To adore it is to adore the Victim who still offers Himself for love of us.

Illustration – A Hidden Adorer

A man who struggled with sin began visiting the Blessed Sacrament daily. Kneeling in silence, he prayed simply: *"Lord, give me strength."* Over time, he discovered that his weakness was being healed at the foot of the tabernacle. Later, he said: *"I found at the altar what I could not find anywhere else — the strength of the Cross alive in the Eucharist."*

His transformation testified that the same power that flowed from Calvary flows still from the altar.

Invitation – Living from the Altar

The Eucharist is not a devotion among others; it is the source and summit of Christian life. To live from the altar is to live from the Cross, drawing strength, healing, and love from Christ's eternal sacrifice.

Ask yourself:

- *Do I approach the Eucharist with the awareness that I am standing at Calvary?*

- *How can I make my Holy Communion an act of deeper surrender to the Crucified Lord?*

- *Am I willing to let the Eucharist shape my life as a continual offering of love?*

Closing Prayer

Lord Jesus, present in the Eucharist, You give me the gift of Calvary made present. Teach me to receive You with reverence, to adore You with love, and to let Your sacrifice become the pattern of my life. May every Communion unite me more deeply to Your Cross and Resurrection. **Amen.**

MEDITATION 15

The Cross and Eternal Life

Reflection – The Doorway to Glory

For the world, death is the end. For the Christian, the Cross has changed everything. The death of Jesus did not close His story; it opened the way to eternal life.

Through the Cross, sin is conquered and heaven's gates are opened. What once was a symbol of defeat has become the key to paradise. Eternal life is not earned by our strength, but given through the wounds of Christ.

Sheen on Death Transformed

> *"Before Calvary, death was a prison with no exit. After Calvary, death became a passage — not an end, but a beginning. In the shadow of the Cross, the grave is no longer dark, for it is illumined by the promise of resurrection."*

Archbishop Sheen taught that the Cross is the hinge of history: it turns death into life, despair into hope, and time into eternity.

Illustration – The Saint's Confidence

St. Thérèse of Lisieux, near her death, whispered: *"I am not dying, I am entering into life."* Her simple words reveal the truth of the Cross: that eternal life is not an abstract hope but a reality secured by Christ's sacrifice.

Her childlike confidence mirrors the invitation given to the good thief: *"This day you will be with Me in paradise."*

Invitation – Living for Eternity

To live in the light of the Cross is to live with eternity in view. Our choices, our sacrifices, and our sufferings take on new meaning when seen as preparation for the life to come.

Ask yourself:

- *Do I live with my eyes fixed on heaven, or only on this passing world?*

- *How does the Cross shape the way I face suffering and even death?*

- *Am I ready to entrust my life to Christ, confident that His Cross has opened eternal life for me?*

Closing Prayer

Jesus, Lord of life and conqueror of death, through Your Cross You have opened heaven for me. Strengthen my faith in the promise of eternal life. Help me to live each day with heaven in mind, carrying my cross with love, until the day I share in Your glory forever. **Amen.**

MEDITATION 16

The Cross and
Christian Discipleship

Reflection – The Mark of a Disciple

When Jesus called His followers, He did not promise comfort or ease. He said plainly: *"If anyone would come after Me, let him deny himself, take up his cross daily, and follow Me."* (Luke 9:23)

Discipleship is not defined by titles or achievements, but by carrying the Cross in union with Christ. To be His disciple is to walk where He walked — along the way of sacrifice, fidelity, and love that costs something.

Sheen on Following the Crucified

> *"Our Lord never promised that following Him would mean escaping the Cross. He promised that it would mean carrying one. The Christian life is not immunity from suffering, but communion in suffering — and through it, communion in love."*

Archbishop Sheen explained that the mark of an authentic disciple is not success in the world's eyes, but the willingness to follow Christ to Calvary.

Illustration – A Modern Witness

A young man once left a lucrative career to enter the seminary. When asked why, he replied: *"I heard Christ say, 'Take up your cross and follow Me.' I realized that if I gave Him everything, I would gain everything."*

His choice reflected the paradox of discipleship: losing one's life in order to find it.

Invitation – Walking the Narrow Way

Every Christian is called to be a disciple, not in word alone but in daily practice. The Cross is the test of that discipleship — not whether we carry it, but how we carry it: with resentment, or with love.

Ask yourself:

- *What cross is Christ asking me to carry today?*

- *Do I see discipleship as convenience, or as sacrifice?*

- *Am I willing to walk behind Him, even when the road leads to Calvary?*

Closing Prayer

Lord Jesus, You call me to follow You on the way of the Cross. Give me courage to deny myself, strength to carry my burdens, and love to persevere to the end. Make me Your disciple, faithful in trial and joyful in sacrifice, until I share the victory of Your Resurrection. **Amen.**

MEDITATION 17

The Cross and the Beatitudes

Reflection – The Sermon on the Mount Fulfilled on Calvary

When Jesus first preached the Beatitudes, He blessed the poor, the meek, the merciful, the pure of heart, the persecuted. On Calvary, He lived them all.

The Cross is the ultimate commentary on the Sermon on the Mount. Poverty of spirit is seen in His surrender. Mercy shines in His forgiveness. Purity of heart is revealed in His obedience. Persecution reaches its climax in His death. The Beatitudes are not ideals for the few, but the way of life for every disciple — a way that leads to the Cross.

Sheen on the Paradox of the Beatitudes

> *"The Beatitudes are not soft virtues for gentle souls; they are the heroic virtues of Christ on the Cross. The world calls them weakness, but Calvary proves them strength. Blessed are the poor, the meek, the merciful — for they are none other than Christ Himself."*

Archbishop Sheen explained that the Beatitudes find their fullest expression at Calvary, where the wisdom of the world is overturned by the wisdom of the Cross.

Illustration – A Hidden Disciple

A missionary once shared the story of a Christian family persecuted for their faith. Despite threats and losses, they remained peaceful, forgiving, and steadfast. *"We would rather lose everything than lose Christ,"* they said.

Their witness reflected the Beatitudes lived in flesh and blood — meekness that was not weakness, mercy that was not naïve, purity of heart that was unshakable.

Invitation – Living the Beatitudes through the Cross

The Beatitudes are not sentimental sayings; they are a road map to Calvary. To live them is to embrace the Cross and to find joy in sacrifice.

Ask yourself:

- *Which Beatitude challenges me the most to live?*

- *How does the Cross give me strength to practice meekness, mercy, or purity of heart?*

- *Am I willing to be "blessed" in the world's eyes as a fool, so that I may be blessed in God's eyes as faithful?*

Closing Prayer

Lord Jesus, You are the living Beatitude, poor in spirit, meek and merciful, pure of heart and persecuted for love. Teach me to live Your words, not as distant ideals, but as a daily Cross. May Your Beatitudes shape my heart, until I reflect Your love to the world. **Amen.**

MEDITATION 18

The Cross and the Church

Reflection – Born from the Side of Christ

When the soldier pierced Christ's side, blood and water flowed forth — signs of Baptism and the Eucharist, the sacramental life of the Church. From the wounded Heart of Christ, the Church was born.

The Cross is not only the foundation of individual salvation but also the origin of the Mystical Body. To belong to the Church is to be united to Christ Crucified, sharing in His sufferings and His mission.

Sheen on the Church of Calvary

> *"The Church is not a society of the perfect but a fellowship of the redeemed, gathered beneath the Cross. Her strength is not her own but flows from the blood that purchased her. To love Christ is to love His Body, the Church."*

Archbishop Sheen taught that the Church is inseparable from the Cross. She draws her life, her holiness, and her mission from Calvary itself.

Illustration – The Faith of the Martyrs

In the early Church, Christians gathered in catacombs, risking their lives to celebrate the Eucharist. They carried within them a profound conviction: *"We cannot live without the Lord's Body and Blood."*

Their witness reminds us that the Church is not sustained by human effort but by the sacrifice of Christ, renewed on every altar.

Invitation – Loving the Church at the Foot of the Cross

To belong to the Church is to share both her glory and her wounds. Like the disciples at Calvary, we are called not to abandon her in times of trial but to stand faithfully by her side.

Ask yourself:

- *Do I see the Church as the wounded yet beloved Bride of Christ?*

- *Am I willing to pray, suffer, and labor for her renewal?*

- *How can I live more consciously as a member of the Body born from the Cross?*

Closing Prayer

Lord Jesus, from Your pierced side flowed the life of the Church. Grant me love for Your Body, fidelity in times of trial, and zeal for her mission. May I never leave the foot of the Cross, but remain with Your Bride, sharing in her sufferings until she shares in Your glory. **Amen.**

MEDITATION 19

The Cross and the Priesthood

Reflection – The Altar of Sacrifice

At the Last Supper, Jesus instituted both the Eucharist and the priesthood. On Calvary, He consummated that gift by offering Himself as the eternal High Priest and Victim. Every priest shares in this mystery: he is ordained not for privilege, but for sacrifice.

The Cross reveals that the priesthood is not a career but a crucifixion. To stand at the altar is to stand at Calvary, offering not only bread and wine, but one's very life in union with Christ.

Sheen on the Priest and the Cross

> *"The priest is called not merely to offer the Cross, but to be on it. Every Mass he celebrates is a personal invitation to die with Christ, that others may live. The world will understand him only when it sees in him the shadow of Calvary."*

Archbishop Sheen insisted that the priesthood cannot be understood apart from sacrifice. The priest is configured to Christ the Victim, and his fruitfulness flows from his willingness to be nailed with Him.

Illustration – A Hidden Shepherd

During persecution in Eastern Europe, priests secretly celebrated the Mass in barns and basements. Many were arrested, some martyred. One survivor later wrote: *"We were not heroes. We were priests. This is what priests do — we offer, even if it costs our lives."*

Their fidelity revealed the essence of the priesthood: to make Christ present through the Cross, no matter the cost.

Invitation – Praying for Priests

Every Christian is called to pray for priests, that they may remain faithful to their vocation of sacrifice. And in a broader sense, every baptized soul shares in Christ's priesthood, called to offer daily life as a spiritual sacrifice to God.

Ask yourself:

- *Do I pray regularly for priests, especially those burdened or tempted?*

- *How can I live my baptismal priesthood by offering my daily crosses in union with Christ?*

- *Am I willing to see the priesthood not only as ministry, but as Calvary made present?*

Closing Prayer

Lord Jesus, Eternal High Priest, sanctify Your priests in the fire of Your love. Grant them fidelity to the Cross, courage in sacrifice, and joy in service. Teach me also, through my baptism, to offer my life as a holy sacrifice, united to Yours at every Mass. **Amen.**

MEDITATION 20

The Cross and Reparation

Reflection – Love That Repairs

Sin is not only the breaking of a law but the wounding of love. Every sin offends the Heart of God. At Calvary, Jesus offered Himself not only to forgive sin but to repair the damage it caused — to restore what was broken, to heal what was wounded, to make love whole again.

Reparation is our response to that love. To make reparation is to console the Heart of Christ by uniting our prayers, sacrifices, and fidelity to His Cross.

Sheen on the Need for Reparation

> *"Sin is not something impersonal; it nailed Him to the Cross. Reparation is not something abstract; it is the return of love for love. To do reparation is to stand with Christ at Calvary and say: 'I will not leave You alone.'"*

Archbishop Sheen explained that reparation is love's answer to the world's indifference. If sin forgets God, reparation remembers Him.

Illustration – The Hidden Consoler

St. Thérèse of Lisieux once said: *"I choose all."* She meant that she would accept every small suffering as a way of consoling Jesus. Whether misunderstood by her sisters or enduring physical pain, she transformed each trial into an act of love.

Her Little Way shows us that reparation is not reserved for great penances; it is lived in hidden fidelity, day by day, for love of Christ.

Invitation – Sharing in Christ's Work

To make reparation is to let our lives become a living "yes" to God's love, repairing the "no" of sin. It may mean offering our sufferings, praying before the Eucharist, or performing small acts of love done with great faith.

Ask yourself:

- *What act of love can I offer today to console the Heart of Christ?*

- *Do I see my daily sacrifices as useless, or as opportunities to repair what sin has wounded?*

- *How can I be a consoler of Jesus in a world that often forgets Him?*

Closing Prayer

O Jesus, You bore the weight of sin upon the Cross. I offer You my prayers, my sacrifices, my love, to console Your Heart and to repair what sin has broken. Teach me to live each day in reparation, that my life may return love for love, until the world is renewed in Your mercy. **Amen.**

MEDITATION 21

The Cross and Hope

Reflection – Light in the Midst of Darkness

From the outside, Calvary looked like defeat. The disciples scattered, the enemies mocked, and the sky itself grew dark. Yet from that darkest hour came the dawn of Easter. The Cross is the paradox of Christian hope: when all seems lost, God is nearest.

Hope does not deny suffering; it transforms it. To hope in the Cross is to believe that God can draw life from death, light from darkness, victory from apparent failure.

Sheen on the Certainty of Hope

> *"Despair sees only the nails; hope sees the hands that are nailed. Despair sees only the thorns; hope sees the brow that wears them as a crown. The Cross is the anchor of hope, because it reveals that God's love is stronger than our sins and greater than our deaths."*

Archbishop Sheen emphasized that hope is not optimism or wishful thinking. It is the confidence that Christ's victory is already won, even when hidden beneath the Cross.

Illustration – A Prisoner's Song

A Christian imprisoned for his faith endured years of darkness with no sign of release. Yet each night, he softly sang hymns of hope. Asked later how he endured, he replied: *"They could chain my body, but not my hope in Christ."*

Like the thief promised paradise, he discovered that even behind bars, the Cross radiates hope that cannot be silenced.

Invitation – Choosing Hope Daily

The Cross confronts us with two choices: despair or hope. To choose hope is to cling to the promises of God when feelings fade, when prayers seem unanswered, when life feels heavy. It is to whisper, "I trust You, Lord," even in the dark.

Ask yourself:

- *Where am I tempted to despair today?*

- *Do I see my Cross as the end of hope, or as the very reason for it?*

- *How can I bear witness to Christian hope in a world that often gives in to despair?*

Closing Prayer

Lord of Calvary and Easter, anchor my heart in hope. When trials weigh me down, lift my eyes to Your Cross. When despair whispers its lies, remind me of Your victory. May I live as a witness that the Cross is never the end, but always the doorway to glory. **Amen.**

MEDITATION 22

The Cross and Love

Reflection – Love Revealed in Full

Love is often spoken of lightly, but on Calvary it is revealed in its truest form. The Cross is love stretched to its limit — a love willing to suffer, to forgive, to give all, holding nothing back.

At the Cross, Jesus shows that love is not sentiment but sacrifice. The measure of love is not how much it feels, but how much it gives.

Sheen on the Measure of Love

> *"The proof of love is sacrifice. He who loves much, suffers much. The Cross is not only the sign of our redemption; it is the sign of what love costs. And unless love costs something, it is not love."*

Archbishop Sheen insisted that the Cross is both revelation and invitation: revelation of how much God loves us, and invitation to love in the same way.

Illustration – A Mother's Gift

A mother who cared for her sick child around the clock was once asked how she found the strength. She replied simply: *"When you love, nothing is too much."*

Her words echoed the heart of Calvary, where Christ gave everything for love, never counting the cost.

Invitation – Learning to Love at the Cross

To live beneath the Cross is to let it redefine love in our lives — in marriages, families, friendships, and communities. Love will always cost something: time, comfort, pride. But in giving, we discover joy.

Ask yourself:

- *Do I measure love by what I receive, or by what I give?*

- *Where is Christ inviting me to love sacrificially today?*

- *Am I willing to let the Cross be the standard of my love?*

Closing Prayer

Crucified Love, teach me to love as You love. Empty me of selfishness, fill me with generosity, and give me the courage to sacrifice with joy. May my love be measured not by words, but by the Cross I bear with You. **Amen.**

MEDITATION 23

The Cross and the Christian Life

Reflection – The Pattern of Every Disciple

The Cross is not only Christ's mission; it is the pattern of the entire Christian life. To follow Him is to take up our own cross daily. Not as punishment, but as participation in His love.

The Christian life is not about avoiding suffering at all costs, but about allowing even our trials to become offerings of love. Calvary becomes the lens through which we see every moment of life — work, family, sacrifice, and prayer.

Sheen on the Christian Vocation

> *"Christianity without a Cross is a lie. Our Lord did not invite us to a path of comfort but to a road of sacrifice. The Christian who would avoid the Cross will avoid Christ Himself, for He is never found apart from it."*

Archbishop Sheen taught that holiness is not achieved by running from suffering, but by embracing it in union with Christ. The Cross is both the cost and the glory of discipleship.

Illustration – A Quiet Witness

A woman caring for her elderly parents once admitted: *"Some days I feel overwhelmed. But when I look at the crucifix, I remember that my small crosses can become prayers, too."*

Her hidden fidelity became a living example of the Christian life: ordinary sacrifice transformed into extraordinary grace by the Cross.

Invitation – Living the Cross Daily

Every Christian is invited to see life itself as a participation in Calvary. The question is not whether we will suffer, but whether we will suffer with Christ or without Him.

Ask yourself:

- *Do I see my daily duties and sacrifices as part of the Cross of Christ?*

- *How can I turn ordinary struggles into offerings of love?*

- *Am I willing to live my whole life in the light of Calvary?*

Closing Prayer

Lord Jesus, make my life a reflection of Your Cross. Let my words, my work, my joys, and my sorrows all be united to You. Teach me to carry my cross daily with love, so that my whole life may proclaim: "I live, now not I, but Christ lives in me." **Amen.**

MEDITATION 24

The Cross and the Saints

Reflection – Holiness Shaped by the Cross

Every saint bears the imprint of Calvary. Their sanctity did not come from escaping suffering, but from embracing it with love. From martyrs in the arena to cloistered nuns in hidden silence, the saints teach us that the Cross is the path to glory.

The Cross purifies, strengthens, and transforms. It is the school where holiness is learned and the fire where love is proved.

Sheen on the Saints of Calvary

> *"The saints are those who loved the Cross, not because suffering is good in itself, but because it is the seal of Christ's love. Every saint has stood at Calvary, some with blood, others with tears, all with love."*

Archbishop Sheen reminded us that sanctity is impossible without the Cross. To admire Christ without sharing His suffering is to stop short of true discipleship.

Illustration – St. Francis and the Crucified

St. Francis of Assisi prayed: *"My God and my all."* His love for the Crucified became so deep that he bore the stigmata — the wounds of Christ in his own body. His life reminds us that the Cross is not distant history but a present reality that can shape a soul completely.

The saints may differ in culture, age, and vocation, but all are united by this: they loved the Cross.

Invitation – Walking the Same Path

Holiness is not reserved for the few but offered to all. The saints prove that the Cross can be carried in every circumstance: in family life, in work, in suffering, in prayer. To imitate them is to join the great procession of souls following Christ to Calvary.

Ask yourself:

- *Do I look to the saints as models of embracing the Cross with love?*

- *Which saint inspires me most to carry my own cross faithfully?*

- *Am I willing to let my trials become the forge of sanctity in my life?*

Closing Prayer

Lord of the saints, You crowned their lives with the glory of the Cross. Teach me to follow their example, to love You in sacrifice, and to remain faithful in trial. May I one day join their company, sharing forever in the victory of Your love. **Amen.**

MEDITATION 25

The Cross and Eternal Glory

Reflection – From Suffering to Splendor

The Cross, once a symbol of shame, has become the throne of glory. By embracing suffering in love, Christ turned death into life and defeat into victory. The wood of the Cross became the ladder to heaven.

For the Christian, this means that every cross carried faithfully is crowned with glory. Our sufferings are not the final word — they are transformed into eternal joy when united with the sacrifice of Christ.

Sheen on Glory Through the Cross

> *"There is no Easter Sunday without Good Friday. The world seeks glory without sacrifice, but Christ shows that glory comes only through the Cross. He who climbs Calvary with Christ will one day share His crown."*

Archbishop Sheen often reminded us that the saints shine brightest because they first embraced the shadows of the Cross. Their eternal reward was born from temporal sacrifice.

Illustration – A Martyr's Crown

St. Ignatius of Antioch, on his way to martyrdom, wrote: *"Let me be ground like wheat in the teeth of wild beasts, that I may become the pure bread of Christ."* His hope was not in escaping suffering, but in the eternal glory that awaited him through the Cross.

His courage shows that the Cross does not diminish life; it enlarges it into eternity.

Invitation – Lifting Our Eyes to Heaven

In moments of trial, the Cross invites us to lift our gaze beyond present pain to the glory to come. Fidelity now prepares us for joy without end.

Ask yourself:

- *Do I see my crosses only as burdens, or also as pathways to eternal glory?*

- *How does the promise of heaven give me strength to endure trials today?*

- *Am I willing to trust that every sacrifice united with Christ will be rewarded in eternity?*

Closing Prayer

Lord of Glory, through the Cross You have opened heaven. Strengthen me to endure my trials with hope, knowing that eternal joy awaits. May every burden I bear in faith be crowned one day with the splendor of Your presence. Let my life proclaim: "Through the Cross to glory."
Amen.

MEDITATION 26

The Cross and Our Daily Mission

Reflection – Sent from Calvary

The Cross does not only call us to faith — it sends us on mission. From the pierced Heart of Christ flowed blood and water, signs of the sacraments through which the Church was born and sent. Every Christian mission begins at Calvary.

To live our mission is to carry the Cross into the world: into homes, workplaces, friendships, and even hostile places. Our witness is not persuasive words alone but lives shaped by sacrificial love.

Sheen on Apostolic Mission

> *"The greatest tragedy in the world is not suffering, but wasted suffering. If we unite our daily trials to the Cross, then they become apostolic — they redeem, they teach, they convert. The Cross carried in love becomes the seed of mission."*

Archbishop Sheen taught that our mission is not apart from the Cross, but born from it. Evangelization is credible when the world sees love that suffers and yet still forgives.

Illustration – A Lay Apostle

A factory worker quietly carried a rosary in his pocket. During breaks, he prayed for his co-workers, offering his long hours as a sacrifice for their souls. Over time, several colleagues returned to the sacraments through his hidden witness.

His mission was not loud or public, but rooted in the Cross lived daily in faithfulness.

Invitation – Carrying the Cross into the World

Each of us has a mission field — our family, workplace, parish, neighborhood. To bring the Cross there is to live sacrificially, to forgive generously, to love when it costs something.

Ask yourself:

- *Where is Christ sending me to be a witness of His Cross?*

- *Do I see my daily struggles as obstacles, or as opportunities for mission?*

- *How can my fidelity become an instrument of grace for others?*

Closing Prayer

Lord Jesus, You sent Your disciples from Calvary to the ends of the earth. Send me into my daily mission with the power of Your Cross. Make my sacrifices fruitful, my prayers apostolic, and my love a witness to Your mercy. May I carry Your Cross into the world, so that others may find life in You. **Amen.**

MEDITATION 27

The Cross and Victory

Reflection – Triumph in Apparent Defeat

On Calvary, Jesus looked like a defeated man: mocked by enemies, abandoned by friends, nailed to a cross. Yet it was precisely there, in the world's darkest hour, that victory was won. Sin was conquered, death was broken, and Satan's power was crushed.

The Cross teaches us that Christian victory does not come through force or domination but through love that suffers and forgives. What looks like loss in the eyes of the world is triumph in the eyes of God.

Sheen on the Paradox of Victory

> *"The world thought it had heard the last of Christ on Calvary. But it was only the beginning. The very act by which His enemies triumphed was the act by which He triumphed over them. The Cross is not failure — it is victory."*

Archbishop Sheen reminded us that the victory of the Cross is quiet yet cosmic, hidden yet eternal. It is the triumph of love over hate, mercy over sin, life over death.

Illustration – A Martyr's Witness

During the early persecutions, Christians often entered the arena singing hymns. To the crowds, their deaths looked like defeat. Yet their joyful surrender inspired conversions across the empire. Their blood became, in Tertullian's famous words, "the seed of the Church."

Their apparent loss was, in truth, the victory of the Cross shining through them.

Invitation – Sharing in Christ's Triumph

We, too, face battles — with sin, discouragement, and temptation. The Cross assures us that victory is already won, though we may not see it yet. Our task is to remain faithful, confident that Christ's triumph will be revealed in us.

Ask yourself:

- *Do I view my struggles as hopeless defeats, or as arenas where Christ's victory can shine?*

- *Am I willing to trust that the Cross has already conquered my greatest fears?*

- *How can I live each day as a witness to Christ's triumph?*

Closing Prayer

Victorious Lord, Your Cross is my hope and my triumph.
Help me to trust that no defeat is final when it is united to You.
Grant me courage in trial, confidence in Your mercy, and joy in the victory of love. May my life proclaim: "The Cross is victory."
Amen.

MEDITATION 28

The Cross and Peace

Reflection – Peace Born from Sacrifice

The world often defines peace as the absence of conflict, comfort, or control. But the Cross reveals a deeper peace — the peace of reconciliation. By His sacrifice, Christ broke down the wall between God and humanity, making peace through the blood of His Cross (Colossians 1:20).

True peace does not ignore suffering; it is born from it. At Calvary, mercy and justice met, and in their embrace, peace was born for the world.

Sheen on Christ the Peace-Maker

"Peace is not merely a truce between enemies; it is the restoration of order through love. Christ brought peace not by avoiding the Cross, but by embracing it. His wounds healed our rebellion, and His death reconciled earth with heaven."

Archbishop Sheen reminded us that peace cannot come from politics, possessions, or power. It flows only from the pierced Heart of Christ.

Illustration – Forgiveness Restores Peace

A man once forgave the drunk driver who had caused the death of his daughter. When asked how, he answered: *"I looked at the crucifix and remembered how much I have been forgiven."*

His act of mercy did not erase his loss, but it gave him peace — the kind of peace that only the Cross can give.

Invitation – Becoming Instruments of Peace

To live beneath the Cross is to become a peacemaker. This does not mean avoiding conflict at any cost, but healing divisions with love and forgiveness. The Cross calls us to bring reconciliation where there is hatred, and hope where there is despair.

Ask yourself:

- *Do I seek peace only in comfort, or in the deeper reconciliation Christ offers?*

- *Where is God asking me to be an instrument of peace — in my family, my parish, my community?*

- *Am I willing to forgive as I have been forgiven?*

Closing Prayer

Lord Jesus, Prince of Peace, by the blood of Your Cross, You reconciled the world to the Father. Heal the divisions in my heart, my family, and my community. Make me an instrument of Your peace, bearing Your mercy where there is hurt, and Your hope where there is despair. Let my life echo Your gift of peace poured out from Calvary. **Amen.**

MEDITATION 29

The Cross and Joy

Reflection – Joy Hidden in Sorrow

At first glance, the Cross seems the opposite of joy. It is a place of pain, loss, and humiliation. Yet hidden within its sorrow is a deeper joy — the joy of love fulfilled, of obedience carried to the end, of redemption accomplished.

Christian joy is not the denial of suffering but the discovery of meaning within it. The Cross shows us that joy and sorrow are not enemies; when united to Christ, sorrow becomes the seed of joy.

Sheen on Joy Through the Cross

"Joy is not the avoidance of the Cross, but the embrace of it. The world promises happiness in pleasures; Christ promises joy in sacrifice. And His promise endures, for the Cross leads not to despair but to resurrection."

Archbishop Sheen explained that Christian joy is the serene confidence that love is stronger than death. It is the peace of knowing that Calvary ends in Easter.

Illustration – Joy in the Midst of Trial

St. Teresa of Calcutta often smiled even in the midst of exhaustion and trial. When asked how, she replied: *"Joy is prayer; joy is strength; joy is love. Joy is love with a smile."*

Her joy was not superficial. It flowed from the Cross — from seeing Christ in the poor, serving Him in sacrifice, and trusting Him in suffering.

Invitation – Choosing Joy in the Cross

Joy is a choice, not a feeling. Each day, we can choose to see the Cross not as an obstacle but as a gift — the place where God's love meets our lives.

Ask yourself:

- *Do I equate joy with comfort, or do I seek it in the love of Christ crucified?*

- *Where can I bring joy into the lives of others through sacrifice and love?*

- *Am I willing to let the Cross transform my sorrows into seeds of joy?*

Closing Prayer

Lord Jesus, You endured the Cross for the joy set before You. Teach me to find joy not in avoiding sacrifice, but in embracing it with love. Let my heart be filled with Easter joy even in Good Friday trials, so that my life may shine with the gladness of the Gospel. **Amen.**

MEDITATION 30

The Cross and the Christian Home

Reflection – The Cross at the Heart of Family Life

The home is often called the "domestic church." It is the place where love is learned, sacrifices are made, and faith is handed on. Yet no home is without its crosses — misunderstandings, hardships, illnesses, or daily struggles.

When the Cross is welcomed into the home, it becomes not a source of division but of unity. Shared sacrifice binds hearts together and opens the door for Christ to dwell in the midst of the family.

Sheen on Family and the Cross

"The Christian home is built not merely on human love but on divine love. And divine love is always marked by the Cross. A family that refuses sacrifice will not endure; a family that embraces it will find strength beyond its own."

Archbishop Sheen taught that the Cross sanctifies family life, transforming ordinary duties into acts of grace and daily struggles into opportunities for holiness.

Illustration – A Family's Hidden Fidelity

A father working two jobs to provide for his children, a mother caring for the sick with patience, siblings learning to forgive quarrels — these may seem small in the world's eyes, but in God's eyes they are acts of Calvary lived at home.

Such hidden sacrifices, offered with love, make the home an altar where Christ's Cross is present and fruitful.

Invitation – Making the Home a Sanctuary of Love

Every home can reflect Calvary by turning sacrifice into love and challenges into opportunities for grace. A crucifix on the wall is not only a decoration but a reminder that Christ is the unseen Guest in every room.

Ask yourself:

- *Do I welcome Christ and His Cross into my home, or do I resist it?*

- *How can I transform daily family sacrifices into offerings of love?*

- *Am I helping my home to be a place where Christ is known, loved, and served?*

Closing Prayer

Lord Jesus, make my home a reflection of Your Cross. Bless my family with patience in trial, forgiveness in conflict, and love in sacrifice. May our home be a sanctuary where Your presence is felt and Your Cross is embraced with faith. **Amen.**

MEDITATION 31

The Cross and the World

Reflection – The Cross as the Axis of History

The Cross is not only the center of Christian life; it is the hinge of history. On Calvary, the world was judged and redeemed. All nations, cultures, and generations must confront its challenge: will we see the Cross as folly, or as the wisdom and power of God (1 Corinthians 1:18)?

The Cross stands above every age, uniting what is good, exposing what is false, and offering hope to a world in need of redemption.

Sheen on the Cross in History

> *"The Cross is the axis around which the universe turns. Empires rise and fall, philosophies come and go, but the Cross endures. It is the one sign that the world cannot escape, for in it lies both its judgment and its salvation."*

Archbishop Sheen often said that the Cross is not only personal but cosmic. It redeems not just individuals but the entire world.

Illustration – The Power of the Cross Across Nations

Missionaries in distant lands have found that even where cultures differ, the Cross speaks a universal language. One missionary told of a village that rejected all foreign customs but welcomed the crucifix, saying: *"This God knows our suffering."*

The Cross is the meeting point where every people and culture can recognize their story fulfilled in Christ.

Invitation – Bearing the Cross for the World

Each Christian is called to see beyond personal salvation to the salvation of the world. By uniting our sacrifices to Christ, we join in His work of redeeming all peoples and nations.

Ask yourself:

- *Do I see the Cross only as my personal consolation, or as God's gift for the whole world?*

- *How can I witness to Christ's love in a culture that often rejects Him?*

- *Am I willing to carry my share of the world's suffering in prayer and sacrifice?*

Closing Prayer

Lord of the nations, Your Cross is the hope of the world. Bring peace where there is war, truth where there is error, and love where there is hatred. Use my life, my prayers, and my sacrifices to extend the shadow of Your Cross across the whole earth, until every knee bows before You. **Amen.**

MEDITATION 32

The Cross and the Christian Apostolate

Reflection – Mission Flows from the Cross

Every apostolate — whether preaching, teaching, serving, or praying — finds its source at Calvary. The apostle is not primarily a strategist or organizer, but a witness to the love poured out on the Cross.

The fruitfulness of any mission does not depend on human talent alone but on union with Christ crucified. Without the Cross, the apostolate becomes activism; with the Cross, it becomes redemptive.

Sheen on Apostolic Zeal

> *"The world is not saved by brilliant men, but by crucified ones. Our Lord chose not the learned of the world, but those willing to leave all and take up their cross. The apostle is great not because of what he does, but because of how much of Christ's Cross he carries."*

Archbishop Sheen reminded us that the power of Christian witness comes from sacrifice. Apostolic zeal is born not of ambition, but of love that is willing to suffer.

Illustration – A Missionary's Secret

A missionary once confessed that the key to his ministry's fruitfulness was not his words, but his hidden hours before the Blessed Sacrament. He said: *"I preached with my lips, but I wept with Christ for souls before the altar. That was my real mission."*

His testimony reveals that the apostolate without prayer and sacrifice is empty, but with the Cross, it becomes life-giving.

Invitation – Making My Life Apostolic

Every Christian is an apostle in some way — in the family, the parish, the workplace, the wider world. Our witness is powerful when it springs from the Cross.

Ask yourself:

- *Do I see my mission as my own work, or as Christ's work through me?*

- *How can I root my apostolic efforts more deeply in prayer and sacrifice?*

- *Am I willing to let my life become a living sermon of the Cross?*

Closing Prayer

Lord of the harvest, make me an apostle of Your Cross. Give me zeal rooted in sacrifice, strength born of prayer, and courage born of love. May all my efforts bear fruit, not for my glory but for Yours, so that the world may know the power of the Cross. **Amen.**

MEDITATION 33

The Cross and the Mystical Body

Reflection – One Body, Sharing One Cross

On Calvary, Christ did not suffer for Himself but for His Body — the Church. By Baptism, we are grafted into Him, made members of His Mystical Body. This means the Cross is no longer His alone; it is ours.

When one member suffers, all suffer; when one is honored, all rejoice (1 Corinthians 12:26). The Cross binds us together in a communion of love, sacrifice, and mission.

Sheen on the Unity of the Body

> *"The Cross is not only Christ's; it belongs to His Body, the Church. Every Christian must fill up what is lacking in the sufferings of Christ — not because His work was incomplete, but because His love is so great that He allows us to share in it."*

Archbishop Sheen emphasized that Christ invites His members to join their sufferings with His, so that His redemptive love may reach every soul.

Illustration – A Chain of Grace

A cloistered nun, unseen by the world, offered her daily sufferings for missionaries in the field. Those missionaries, in turn, brought the Gospel to villages that had never heard of Christ. Souls were saved because one hidden member of the Body carried her cross in love.

Her example shows how the Cross unites us in a chain of grace that stretches across the world.

Invitation – Sharing in the Sufferings of Christ

To belong to the Mystical Body is to bear one another's burdens, offering our crosses not only for ourselves but for the salvation of others.

Ask yourself:

- *Do I see my sufferings as isolated, or as joined to the Body of Christ?*

- *Whom can I consciously carry in prayer through the weight of my cross?*

- *Am I willing to unite my sacrifices to Christ for the sake of His Church?*

Closing Prayer

Lord Jesus, Head of the Body, teach me to suffer and to love with You. Unite my small crosses to Your great sacrifice, so that grace may flow to others. Make me a faithful member of Your Mystical Body, sharing in its sorrows and its joys, until we are one with You in glory. **Amen.**

MEDITATION 34

The Cross and the Sacraments

Reflection – Channels from Calvary

When Jesus died on the Cross, blood and water flowed from His pierced side — signs of the sacraments that would spring forth from His sacrifice. Baptism cleanses us in that water, the Eucharist nourishes us with that blood, and the other sacraments draw their power from the same fountain of grace.

The sacraments are not human rituals but divine streams flowing directly from Calvary, carrying the fruits of redemption into every generation.

Sheen on the Sacramental Life

> *"The Cross is the fountainhead of the sacraments. They are the continuation of Calvary through time. Each sacrament applies the fruits of the Passion to our souls, making us contemporaries of the saving act of Christ."*

Archbishop Sheen emphasized that the sacraments unite us to the Cross in real, tangible ways. In every Baptism, Confirmation, Confession, Eucharist, Matrimony, Ordination, and Anointing, Calvary is present.

Illustration – The Power of Confession

A man burdened by years of sin entered the confessional with trembling. When the priest pronounced absolution, he later said: *"I felt as if the weight of the Cross itself had lifted me up."*

His experience reflected the truth that in every sacrament, the grace of the Cross touches individual lives with healing and power.

Invitation – Living from the Sacraments

The sacraments are not optional extras but the ordinary means by which we live the mystery of the Cross. To receive them is to drink from the side of Christ and to be renewed in His sacrifice.

Ask yourself:

- *Do I approach the sacraments as routine, or as encounters with the Cross?*

- *How can I deepen my preparation and thanksgiving for each sacrament I receive?*

- *Am I letting the grace of Calvary, poured out in the sacraments, transform my daily life?*

Closing Prayer

Lord Jesus, from Your pierced side flowed the sacraments of the Church. Grant me reverence when I approach them, gratitude when I receive them, and fidelity in living their grace. Through them, may my life be ever united to Your Cross and open to Your Resurrection. **Amen.**

MEDITATION 35

The Cross and Mary

Reflection – The Mother at Calvary

No one stood closer to the mystery of the Cross than Mary. She shared not in the physical nails or scourging, but in the agony of a pierced heart. At Calvary, she became not only the Mother of Jesus but the Mother of all the redeemed.

Her presence at the Cross reminds us that discipleship is not only about doing, but about standing — remaining faithful, even when the sword pierces the soul.

Sheen on Mary at the Cross

"Mary was not merely a spectator at Calvary. She was a co-sufferer. As Jesus gave His Body, she gave her Son. As He offered His life, she offered her maternal heart. In her we see the perfect disciple who never turned away from the Cross."

Archbishop Sheen taught that Mary's greatest act of faith was not at Nazareth, but at Calvary — trusting God even when His plan seemed most hidden.

Illustration – A Mother's Silent Strength

A mother caring for her son battling addiction once said: *"I cannot take his cross away, but I can stand beside him."*

Her words echo Mary at Calvary, who could not remove the nails but could remain faithful. Her silent strength became her son's greatest consolation.

Invitation – Taking Mary into Our Lives

From the Cross, Jesus entrusted Mary to John, and John to Mary. Each of us is invited to do the same — to take her into our homes, our hearts, our struggles. She teaches us how to remain at the Cross without despair and how to love even in suffering.

Ask yourself:

- *Have I welcomed Mary as my Mother, especially in times of trial?*

- *Do I turn to her for consolation and strength at the foot of my own crosses?*

- *Am I willing to let her teach me how to stand faithfully with Christ?*

Closing Prayer

Mary, Mother of Sorrows, teach me to stand with you at the Cross. Help me to offer my sufferings with love, to trust when I do not understand, and to remain faithful when trials come. Be my Mother, my comfort, and my guide, until I share forever in the victory of your Son. **Amen.**

MEDITATION 36

The Cross and the Mass

Reflection – Calvary Made Present

The Mass is not a mere remembrance of Calvary, but its living presence. At every altar, the sacrifice of the Cross is renewed in an unbloody manner. We are not transported back in time; rather, the mystery of Calvary is brought into our time and place.

To attend Mass, then, is to stand once more at the foot of the Cross with Mary and John. It is to see love poured out and to join our lives to that offering.

Sheen on the Mass as Sacrifice

> *"The Mass is Calvary without distance of space or time. The same Christ is present, the same sacrifice is offered, the same love is poured out. The difference is only this: on Calvary He was alone; at the Mass we are invited to offer ourselves with Him."*

Archbishop Sheen insisted that the Mass is not primarily about receiving, but about offering — uniting our lives, joys, and sorrows with Christ's perfect oblation.

Illustration – A Hidden Offering

A parishioner once whispered before Mass: *"I place my whole week on the altar."* Her struggles at work, her worries for her children, her hidden sacrifices — all became part of the bread and wine, lifted up with Christ's Cross to the Father.

Her witness reveals that when we unite our lives to the Mass, nothing is wasted.

Invitation – Living the Mass Beyond the Altar

The Mass does not end at the dismissal; it begins anew in our daily lives. What we have offered at the altar, we must live in the world. To live Eucharistically is to carry the Cross into every corner of life.

Ask yourself:

- *Do I approach Mass as a true encounter with Calvary, or only as a ritual?*

- *What can I consciously place on the altar at my next Mass?*

- *Am I living what I celebrate — making my life an offering united to Christ's?*

Closing Prayer

Lord Jesus, at every Mass You renew the gift of Calvary. Teach me to come with reverence, to offer myself with You, and to live each day as a Eucharistic sacrifice. May I never forget that the altar is the Cross, and that in Your sacrifice I find my life. **Amen.**

MEDITATION 37

The Cross and Christian Virtue

Reflection – Virtue Tested in Fire

Virtue is not formed in comfort but in trial. Patience, humility, courage, and charity grow when tested by the weight of the Cross. Calvary is the forge where Christian virtue is purified and perfected.

The Cross shows us that virtue is not simply about self-improvement but about self-giving. It is love in action, even when it costs something.

Sheen on Virtue from the Cross

> *"The virtues are not abstract qualities but Christ Himself living in us. Patience is His patience in our trials, humility is His humility in our struggles, charity is His charity in our sacrifices. Virtue flows not from willpower alone but from union with the Cross."*

Archbishop Sheen taught that the Cross transforms natural strengths into supernatural virtues by rooting them in love.

Illustration – Patience in Trial

A man caring for his bedridden wife was once asked how he bore the burden. He answered: *"Every day I look at the crucifix and remember: love is patient. If He endured for me, I can endure for her."*

His patience was not weakness but strength born at Calvary — a living virtue shaped by the Cross.

Invitation – Practicing Virtue Daily

Every day brings opportunities to grow in virtue: to choose humility over pride, forgiveness over resentment, patience over anger, generosity over selfishness. The Cross makes these choices possible by giving us the strength of Christ Himself.

Ask yourself:

- *Which virtue is God asking me to cultivate right now?*

- *Do I rely only on my own strength, or do I draw from the grace of the Cross?*

- *How can I practice small acts of virtue each day, rooted in love?*

Closing Prayer

Lord Jesus, You are the perfection of every virtue. Form in me patience, humility, courage, and charity through the trials I face. May the Cross be my teacher, and may my life reflect Your virtues, until I shine with Your likeness. **Amen.**

MEDITATION 38

The Cross and the Christian Nation

Reflection – A People Under the Cross

Nations, like individuals, rise or fall by how they relate to the Cross. A Christian nation is not one without suffering, but one that interprets its trials in the light of Calvary. When the Cross is honored, justice and mercy flourish; when it is rejected, selfishness and division reign.

The health of a society is measured not by wealth or power but by whether it is willing to sacrifice for the common good, just as Christ sacrificed for all.

Sheen on the Cross and Society

> *"The Cross is not only the salvation of souls but the salvation of civilization. A nation that forgets the Cross will die of its own selfishness; a nation that remembers it will endure through sacrifice and love."*

Archbishop Sheen warned that when societies abandon the Cross, they also abandon truth and charity. But when they embrace it, they are renewed in justice, compassion, and peace.

Illustration – Renewal in Hardship

After a devastating war, a small village rebuilt its church, beginning with the crucifix that had survived the destruction. Families carried stones, children gathered wood, elders prayed aloud. That crucifix reminded them that only through the Cross could their community be restored.

Their faith bore witness that the Cross is not only personal but national, capable of renewing whole peoples.

Invitation – Bearing the Cross for the Common Good

As Christians, we are called to bring the Cross into our civic life — through honesty, sacrifice, service, and the defense of truth. A nation grows strong when its citizens live the virtues of Calvary.

Ask yourself:

- *Do I see my role in society as shaped by the Cross?*

- *How can I bring sacrificial love into my community and nation?*

- *Am I willing to suffer for truth and justice, even when unpopular?*

Closing Prayer

Lord of nations, place my country beneath the shadow of Your Cross. Heal our divisions, renew our leaders in wisdom, and strengthen our people in virtue. May we be a nation willing to sacrifice for love, and may the Cross be our guide and our glory. **Amen.**

MEDITATION 39

The Cross and Perseverance

Reflection – Enduring to the End

The Christian life is not a sprint but a pilgrimage. Along the way, many grow weary, some turn back, and others stumble. The Cross teaches us that victory is not found in starting well, but in finishing faithfully.

Jesus carried His Cross to the very end. Perseverance is the virtue of remaining steady beneath the weight of trial until love has completed its work.

Sheen on Perseverance at Calvary

> *"Our Lord did not come down from the Cross when taunted. He endured until the sacrifice was complete. Perseverance is the mark of true love — not to love only when it is easy, but to love until the very end."*

Archbishop Sheen reminded us that perseverance is the proof of authentic faith. To endure faithfully in trials is to mirror Christ's own fidelity.

Illustration – A Steadfast Soul

A woman who prayed daily for her wayward son did not give up, even after decades without change. Near the end of her life, he returned to the sacraments. She said simply: *"I just kept carrying the cross for him."*

Her perseverance reflected the patient endurance of Calvary, where love refuses to give up.

Invitation – Remaining Faithful in Trial

The Cross invites us to steadfastness. Perseverance is not stubbornness but fidelity — the refusal to abandon Christ when the road grows hard.

Ask yourself:

- *Where am I tempted to give up in faith, prayer, or duty?*

- *Do I carry my cross only when light, or also when heavy?*

- *Am I willing to endure to the end, trusting in Christ's victory?*

Closing Prayer

Lord Jesus, You persevered to the end upon the Cross. Strengthen me when I grow weary, sustain me when I am tempted to quit, and keep me faithful in love. May I finish the race, carry the Cross to the end, and share in the crown of life You promise. **Amen.**

MEDITATION 40

The Cross and Final Perseverance

Reflection – The Grace of a Faithful End

Life is filled with many beginnings, but what matters most is how we end. Final perseverance is the grace to remain faithful to Christ until our last breath. At Calvary, Jesus showed us how to die — not in despair, but in surrender, entrusting His spirit into the Father's hands.

The Cross teaches us that the Christian's last act is not defeat but offering — returning our life to the One who gave it.

Sheen on Persevering to the End

> *"In the end, men are judged not by the beginnings of their lives but by their closings. Judas began well, Peter began poorly; but Peter ended well, and Judas ended badly. Final perseverance is the crowning grace, and it is won at the foot of the Cross."*

Archbishop Sheen reminded us that no matter how weak our past has been, the grace of final perseverance is always possible — if we remain close to the Crucified.

Illustration – A Holy Death

A priest once kept vigil at the bedside of a dying woman. Though she had suffered much, her final words were: *"Into Your hands, O Lord."* With the crucifix in her hand, she surrendered her spirit in peace.

Her holy death bore witness that the Cross prepares us not only for life but for eternity.

Invitation – Preparing for the Last Hour

Every day is preparation for the final surrender. To live well is to die well. If we carry our crosses faithfully in life, we will be ready to place them down at the feet of Christ in death.

Ask yourself:

- *Am I preparing daily for the moment I will entrust my spirit to the Father?*

- *Do I pray for the grace of final perseverance — for myself and for others?*

- *How can I live now in such a way that my death will be a final act of love?*

Closing Prayer

Lord Jesus, grant me the grace of final perseverance. Keep me faithful to Your Cross until my last breath. When my hour comes, receive my spirit into the Father's hands. Let my death be a prayer of love, united to Yours upon the Cross, and open the gates of eternal life. **Amen.**

MEDITATION 41

The Cross and Eternal Salvation

Reflection – The Price of Our Redemption

At Calvary, Jesus paid the full price for our salvation. No human effort, no act of merit, could open the gates of heaven. Only the Blood of the Lamb, poured out on the Cross, could redeem us.

Eternal salvation is not a reward we earn but a gift we receive — won at a great cost. The Cross is the key that unlocks eternity, the bridge between earth and heaven.

Sheen on Salvation Through the Cross

> *"There is no salvation apart from the Cross. All who are saved are saved by it — whether they know it or not. The Cross is the one bridge from time to eternity, the one ladder reaching from earth to heaven."*

Archbishop Sheen explained that the Cross is not merely a symbol of salvation, but its very source. It is the fountain from which grace flows to every soul.

Illustration – A Soul Saved at the End

A man estranged from the Church for decades received the Sacraments on his deathbed. Holding the crucifix, he whispered: *"This is my passport to heaven."* His final act of faith showed that salvation rests not in our achievements, but in the mercy of Christ crucified.

Invitation – Living in the Light of Salvation

To know that Christ has won eternal life for us should transform how we live. Salvation is already offered; our task is to accept it, live it, and share it with others.

Ask yourself:

- *Do I truly believe that my salvation was purchased on Calvary?*

- *How do I live in gratitude for such a costly gift?*

- *Am I helping others discover the hope of eternal salvation in the Cross?*

Closing Prayer

Saviour of the world, by Your Cross You have redeemed us. I thank You for the gift of eternal life, purchased at such a price. Keep me faithful to Your love, grateful for Your mercy, and eager to share the hope of salvation with others, until I see You face to face in glory. **Amen.**

MEDITATION 42

The Cross and Eternity

Reflection – The Eternal Sign of Love

The Cross is not only the center of history but the center of eternity. In heaven, the wounds of Christ remain — not as scars of defeat, but as trophies of love. For all eternity, the redeemed will gaze upon the Lamb who was slain and worship the One who loved them unto death.

The Cross reminds us that eternity is not an escape from suffering but the fulfillment of love. What was begun in sacrifice on Calvary will shine forever in glory.

Sheen on the Eternal Cross

> *"The Cross will never pass away. Time may roll on, empires may crumble, the stars themselves may fade, but the Cross will endure as the eternal proof of God's love. It will be the song of the blessed and the judgment of the lost."*

Archbishop Sheen explained that in eternity, the Cross will remain the central mystery — the measure of love and the source of unending joy.

Illustration – A Saint's Vision

St. John, in the Book of Revelation, saw a vision of heaven: the Lamb standing as though slain, surrounded by angels and saints singing: *"Worthy is the Lamb who was slain."* (Revelation 5:12) Eternity is nothing less than the endless contemplation and adoration of Christ crucified and risen.

Invitation – Living for the Eternal Cross

If the Cross is the center of eternity, then it must also be the center of our lives now. To carry our crosses faithfully is to prepare our souls for the unending joy of heaven.

Ask yourself:

- *Do I see my crosses as temporary burdens or as preparations for eternal glory?*

- *Am I learning now to love the Cross, so that I may rejoice in it forever?*

- *How can I live today with my eyes fixed on eternity?*

Closing Prayer

Eternal Lord, Your Cross is my hope on earth and my joy in heaven. Teach me to carry it faithfully now, so that I may adore it eternally with the saints. May the song of my heart echo forever: "Worthy is the Lamb who was slain." **Amen.**

MEDITATION 43

Conclusion: The Cross and the Christian Soul

Reflection – The Soul at Calvary

Every soul stands before the Cross with a choice: to reject it as folly or to embrace it as salvation. The Cross is not only Christ's; it is ours. It marks us, shapes us, and leads us into the mystery of God's love.

To live as a Christian soul is to live in the shadow of Calvary, carrying the Cross daily, trusting in its power, and longing for the glory it promises.

Sheen on the Cross as Personal

> *"The Cross is not something outside of us. It is within us. We cannot look upon Calvary and say: 'That is His Cross, not mine.' For every Christian soul, the Cross is both burden and blessing, both weight and wing. It is the only way to heaven."*

Archbishop Sheen often reminded the faithful that the Cross is not an accessory to Christianity but its essence. Without the Cross, there is no Christ; without Christ, no salvation.

Illustration – A Life Transformed

A young woman once testified: *"When I first looked at the Cross, I saw only suffering. Now I see love. It has changed everything — how I pray, how I forgive, how I live."*

Her journey mirrors that of every soul who learns to see in the Cross not defeat but the face of God's mercy.

Invitation – Making the Cross My Own

The conclusion of every meditation on the Cross is not knowledge but transformation. Each of us is invited to take up our cross and follow Christ, letting it shape our soul into His likeness.

Ask yourself:

- *Do I see the Cross as a distant event, or as the daily pattern of my life?*

- *Am I willing to let the Cross define my identity as a Christian soul?*

- *Will I embrace it not only as burden, but as the greatest gift of love?*

Closing Prayer

Lord Jesus, Your Cross is my salvation and my crown. Engrave it upon my soul, that I may never be separated from it. Teach me to love it, to carry it, to live it, until it leads me home to You. May my soul always rest in the shadow of the Cross, and rise one day in the light of Your Resurrection. **Amen.**

EPILOGUE

Living the Fruits of the Cross

The Cross does not end with death. It bears fruit in resurrection, in holiness, and in the transformation of those who take it to heart. To meditate on the Seven Last Words is not merely to remember what Christ has done, but to be changed by it — to let the mystery of Calvary shape the way we live each day.

Archbishop Fulton J. Sheen often reminded us that the Cross is not just a place of suffering, but a school of virtue. Each Word spoken from Calvary teaches us how to overcome sin, how to grow in holiness, and how to live the Beatitudes with greater fidelity.

- *"Father, forgive them"* calls us to overcome anger with mercy.

- *"Today you will be with Me in Paradise"* invites us to turn from despair to hope.

- *"Behold your mother"* teaches us to reject isolation and embrace communion with Mary and the Church.

- *"My God, why have You forsaken Me?"* strengthens us to endure desolation with trust.

- *"I thirst"* compels us to overcome indifference with love.

- *"It is finished"* inspires us to persevere in fidelity to our mission.

- *"Father, into Your hands I commit My spirit"* shows us how to die — and how to live — in surrender to God.

The Beatitudes, too, are lived at the foot of the Cross. Poverty of spirit, meekness, hunger for righteousness, purity of heart, mercy, peace, and perseverance in persecution — all of these shine in the Passion of Christ. What He lived perfectly, we are invited to live imperfectly but faithfully.

To practice virtue, then, is not to imitate an abstract ideal but to follow the Crucified One. Each time we choose humility over pride, patience over anger, purity over lust, generosity over selfishness, we are living the fruits of Calvary. Each act of virtue becomes an echo of His sacrifice, a small share in His redemption, a step toward the Beatitudes.

The Cross is not the end of life but the beginning of a new way of living. It is not a burden to be carried alone but a ladder to Heaven, a path of love that transforms us from within. To meditate on the Seven Last Words is to hear Christ's voice speaking into every part of our lives, calling us not just to adore Him, but to follow Him.

May these meditations bear fruit in you. May they strengthen you to practice virtue, to overcome sin, and to live the Beatitudes. And may you, at life's end, be able to say with Christ: *"It is finished."*

Guide to Making a
Holy Hour at Calvary

The Holy Hour is an invitation to watch and pray with Jesus in His Passion, uniting ourselves with Him at Calvary. Archbishop Fulton J. Sheen called the daily Holy Hour the "hour of power." For over sixty years of priesthood, he spent one hour each day before the Blessed Sacrament, drawing strength for his preaching and intimacy for his soul. He urged every Christian to do the same.

This guide is offered to help you enter into prayer at the foot of the Cross, uniting your Holy Hour to Calvary.

Preparation

Choose a quiet place: before the Blessed Sacrament, in an Adoration Chapel, or before a crucifix at home.

Silence your phone and set aside distractions.

Ask the Holy Spirit to help you enter deeply into the mystery of the Cross.

1. Begin in Silence

Kneel before the crucifix or the Blessed Sacrament. Make an act of adoration and recollection.

Opening Prayer (2–3 minutes)

Begin with a prayer inviting the Lord to be with you:

Lord Jesus, I come to be with You in this hour.
You are my crucified King, my Savior, my Friend.
Teach me to love You as You have loved me.
Amen.

2. Read from Scripture(5–7 minutes)

Read one of the Passion narratives:

- Matthew 26–27

- Mark 14–15

- Luke 22–23

- John 18–19

Pause and let a word or phrase remain in your heart. Let the words draw you into Christ's suffering love.

3. Meditate on the Seven Last Words (15-20 minutes)

Take one Word at a time, reflecting on each Word slowly, recalling the meditations in this book. Pause to reflect on how it applies to your own life and how you can make reparation

4. Intercessory Prayer (10 minutes)

At the foot of the Cross, place before Jesus:

Your own needs.
The needs of loved ones.
The needs of the Church and the world.

Pray with Mary

Pray the Rosary or a Marian hymn, standing with Our Lady at the foot of the Cross. Ask her to help you share in her fidelity and compassion.

Offer Reparation

Bring before Christ the sins of the world — your own, those of your family, the Church, and all humanity. Whisper acts of love to console His Sacred Heart.

5. Contemplative Silence (10 minutes)

Simply remain with Him.

Gaze upon the Crucifix or the Blessed Sacrament, aware of His love and presence.

Rest in His Presence

Allow silence to speak. Listen. Offer your heart. Remember Sheen's words: *"The greatest love story of all time is contained in a tiny white Host."*

6. Conclude with Thanksgiving (5 minutes)

End with a prayer of gratitude for the gift of the Cross. Ask for the grace to carry your daily crosses in union with His.

Pray in your own words, or use this act of entrustment:

Father, into Your hands I commit my spirit,
my heart, my past, my present, my future.
May Your will be done in me,
as it was in Jesus at Calvary.
Amen.

Additional Practices during the Holy Hour (Optional)

- Pray the Stations of the Cross during the hour.

- Sing or pray a Passion hymn.

- Write a short letter to Jesus expressing your love and gratitude.

Encouragement from Fulton Sheen:

> *"The purpose of the Holy Hour is not to change God, but to change us. It is to conform our lives to the will of Him who loved us to the end."*

Practical Note: *Even if you cannot make a full sixty minutes, begin with what you can. Ten, fifteen, or thirty minutes of faithful prayer will bear fruit if offered with love.*

CONCLUDING WORD
Sent from Calvary

You have walked through these pages as through a retreat — listening at Calvary, kneeling at the foot of the Cross, and hearing once again the Seven Last Words of Our Lord. Along the way, you have stood with the Blessed Mother, Mary and St. John, prayed with the saints, and discovered how the mystery of the Cross touches every part of life: our sufferings, our joys, our families, our vocations, our sins, our virtues, and our hopes.

The Cross is not only a moment in history; it is the pattern of discipleship. Every nail and thorn tells us of love. Every word spoken from the wood of the cross is spoken to you personally. The same Jesus who cried "I thirst" still thirsts for your love today; the same Lord who entrusted His Spirit to the Father now invites you to place your whole life into those same hands.

Do not be afraid to return often to Calvary. Make it the place of your prayer, the measure of your love, and the strength of your mission. In the Cross you will find healing for wounds, pardon for sins, and hope for eternal life. In the Cross, you will also discover your own calling — to live, suffer, forgive, and rejoice with Christ until He comes again in glory.

As Archbishop Fulton Sheen reminded us: *"Unless there is a Good Friday in your life, there will never be an Easter Sunday."* May this book be not only a companion for meditation but a seed of transformation. May you leave these pages renewed in faith, strengthened in hope, and on fire with love.

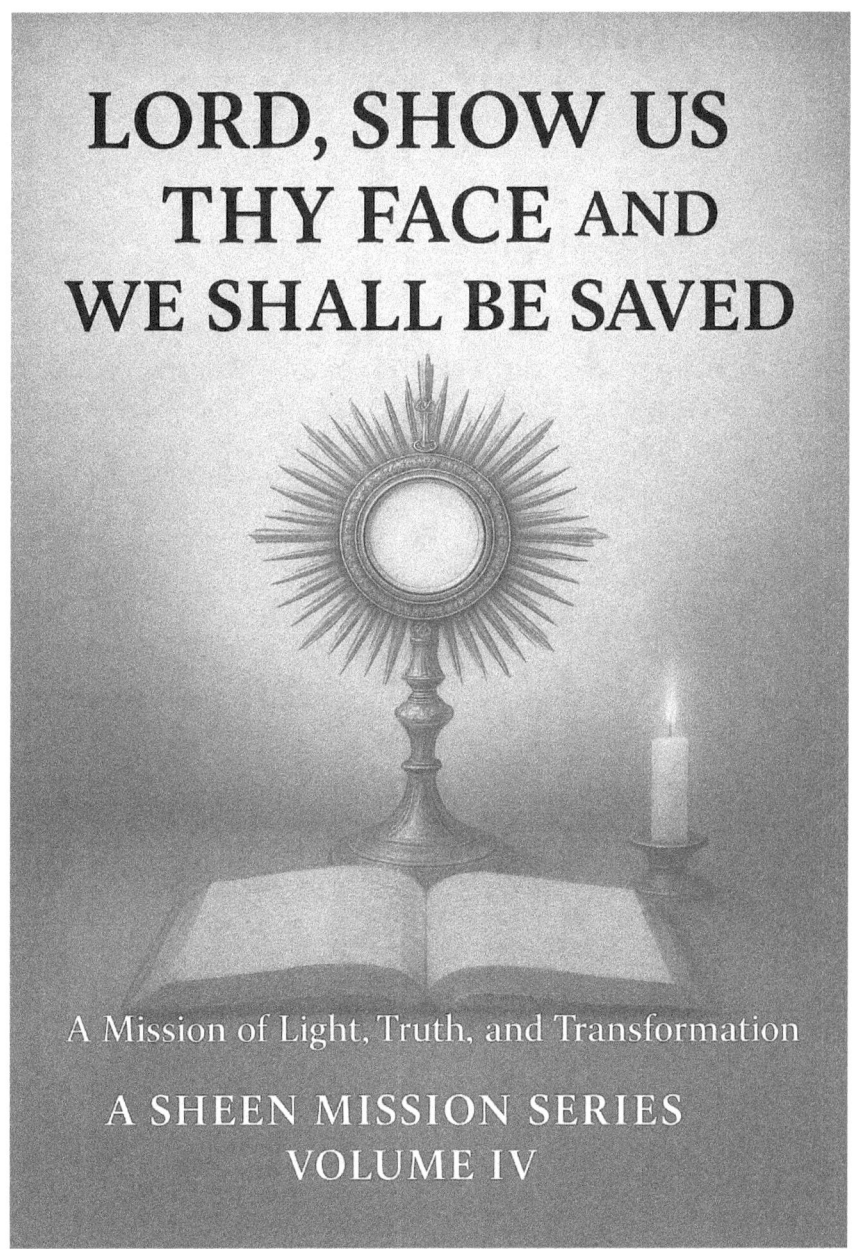

LORD, SHOW US
THY FACE AND
WE SHALL BE SAVED

A Mission of Light, Truth, and Transformation

A SHEEN MISSION SERIES
VOLUME IV

LORD, SHOW US THY FACE AND WE SHALL BE SAVED

A Mission of Light, Truth, and Transformation
A Sheen Mission Series — Volume IV

The Sheen Mission Series invites you to walk with Archbishop Fulton J. Sheen in prayer, reparation, and renewal — a journey of the Holy Face, the Cross, the Eucharist, and Our Blessed Mother.

Description:

*L*ord, *Show Us Thy Face and We Shall Be Saved* is the fourth volume in the Sheen Mission Series — a mission of light, truth, and transformation centred on the Eucharist and the Face of Christ.

This book gathers Sheen's reflections on Eucharistic adoration, the call to reparation, and the power of Christ's Face to renew hearts and heal the world. It is both a prayer manual and a missionary summons — inviting every soul to be transformed by the radiance of Christ's presence.

> *"The Face of Christ is the Gospel made visible. To contemplate His Face is to contemplate the love that saves the world."*

> **— Archbishop Fulton J. Sheen**

Preface

There is a prayer that rises like incense from the pages of the Psalms: *"Restore us, O Lord; let Your Face shine, that we may be saved."* (Psalm 80:3) It is a prayer that expresses the deepest longing of the human heart — the desire to see God, to be seen by Him, and to live in the light of His countenance.

This volume, the fourth and final in the *Sheen Mission Series*, is built upon that cry. It is a meditation on the Face of Christ — the Face that reveals the invisible God, the Face that shone in Bethlehem, wept in Gethsemane, bled on Calvary, and now radiates in glory from the Eucharist. To seek His Face is to seek salvation. To contemplate His countenance is to find peace.

Archbishop Fulton J. Sheen, whose life and teaching inspire this series, never tired of proclaiming that Christianity is not an idea but a Person — the living Christ who meets us face to Face. In every Holy Hour, Sheen adored that Face hidden in the Eucharist, and from that contemplation drew the strength to preach Christ to millions. He understood that evangelization begins in adoration, and that the transformation of the world begins with the transformation of the soul before God.

This book follows that path. It begins with the revelation of Christ's Face in the Incarnation, shines with the radiance of the Eucharist, and leads us through the mystery of reparation, the darkness of the Cross, the light of the Church, and the quiet transformation of contemplation. Each chapter is a step along the way of seeking His countenance more deeply, so that we may also reflect it more faithfully to others.

The *Sheen Mission Series* began with the **Holy Face and the Little Way**, guiding us with St. Thérèse of Lisieux to console and love Christ in reparation. It led us to **Behold Your Mother**, where Mary's sorrowful and tender gaze taught us to stand at the foot of the Cross. It brought us to **The Cross and the Last Words**, where Sheen himself became our companion at Calvary, opening the treasures of Christ's dying words. And now, in this final volume, it gathers all together in a single plea: *"Lord, show us Thy Face, and we shall be saved."*

This is not merely a conclusion but a sending forth. To contemplate the Face of Christ is to be changed by it. And to be changed by it is to become His Face in the world — radiant with His love, merciful in His name, and steadfast in His truth.

May this book, like the series it completes, draw you into a deeper intimacy with Our Lord. May it inspire you to spend time before His Eucharistic countenance. May it strengthen you in reparation, in mission, in suffering, and in joy. And above all, may it awaken in your heart the great longing that will only be satisfied when at last we see Him face to Face in glory.

Foreword

A t the heart of the Church is a mystery both hidden and revealed: the Eucharist. Behind the silence of the tabernacle, behind the veils of bread and wine, dwells the living Christ — His Face radiant with mercy, His Heart burning with love.

Archbishop Fulton J. Sheen often declared that "The greatest love story of all time is contained in a tiny white Host." For over sixty years, he lived this love story daily by keeping a Holy Hour before the Blessed Sacrament. He urged priests, religious, and laypeople alike to do the same, convinced that the renewal of the Church and the healing of the world would come through Eucharistic adoration.

This book — the fourth in the Sheen Mission Series — continues that call. It is an invitation to discover anew the transforming power of the Eucharist, to see the Face of Christ in the Host, and to allow His Presence to change your life.

Sheen reminded us that before we can bring Christ to others, we must first spend time with Him ourselves. Adoration is not wasted time; it is the source of all fruitfulness. From silence before the Eucharist flows strength for mission, clarity for discernment, and courage for sacrifice.

May these pages draw you into that silence, where the Face of Christ shines most brightly. And may they help you discover what Sheen himself discovered: that in adoration, we do not merely look at Christ — we are looked upon by Him.

Introduction

Why the Eucharist? Why Now?

W hy the Eucharist? Because it is Christ Himself, given to us as food for the journey. Because in the Host, we encounter the same Jesus who walked the roads of Galilee, who died upon the Cross, and who now reigns in glory. The Eucharist is not a symbol, but the living Presence of the Lord, Emmanuel — God with us.

Why now? Because our world is starving. In an age of noise, distraction, and unbelief, countless souls long for meaning and intimacy but seek it in places that cannot satisfy. Archbishop Sheen saw clearly that "the world is not dying for want of knowledge; it is dying for want of love." That love is found, above all, in the Eucharist.

This fourth volume in the Sheen Mission Series brings together reflections and prayers that lead us to the altar, the monstrance, and the tabernacle. Its aim is threefold:

- To foster a deeper love for the Eucharist as the center of Christian life.

- To encourage regular adoration before the Blessed Sacrament.

- To inspire a spirit of mission, bringing Christ's light and truth into the world.

It is my prayer that this book will help you fall in love with Christ anew in the Eucharist. May you discover, in the silence of adoration, that the Face of Christ shines not only upon the altar, but also upon your heart.

For the words of the Psalmist remain true: "Let Your Face shine, that we may be saved." (Psalm 80:3)

The Light of His Face

There is a cry that runs through all of Scripture: *"Let Your face shine upon us, Lord, and we shall be saved."* (Psalm 80:3) From the Old Testament psalmist to the disciples who longed to see Christ, the human heart has always yearned for the Face of God. In Jesus Christ, that longing is fulfilled. His is the Face that reveals the invisible God, the countenance that radiates mercy, the visage that endured spittle and thorns, and the glory that shines brighter than the sun at His Resurrection.

Archbishop Fulton J. Sheen often reminded us that Christianity is not a philosophy, but a Person — a living Christ who gazes upon us in love. To contemplate His Face is to enter into that love. To adore Him in the Eucharist is to be bathed in the radiance of His presence. To make reparation is to console the Face that was disfigured for our sake.

This volume, the final in the *Sheen Mission Series*, is both a prayer and a summons. It is an invitation to let the Eucharist become the light of your soul, to see in Mary the reflection of her Son's Face, and to bring that radiance into the darkness of the world. It is a call to reparation, but also to transformation. For when the world looks upon our lives, it must not see us alone — it must see the Face of Christ shining through us.

Let us then take up the ancient cry: *"Lord, show us Thy Face, and we shall be saved."*

MEDITATION 1

The Face of Christ Revealed

Before the coming of Christ, the world could only glimpse the Face of God in shadows and signs. Moses, who spoke with God as a friend, was told: *"You cannot see My Face, for man shall not see Me and live."* (Exodus 33:20) And yet, from that moment, the prophets continued to speak of a day when the light of God's countenance would be revealed to His people.

In the Incarnation, this promise is fulfilled. The eternal Word takes flesh, and for the first time in history, the Face of God is visible. The Child of Bethlehem, wrapped in swaddling clothes, bears the same countenance that will later shine on Mount Tabor and bleed on Calvary. To gaze upon the Infant is already to gaze upon the Redeemer.

Archbishop Fulton J. Sheen often said that God became visible so that we might fall in love with Him. The eyes of Christ look upon us not with judgment but with mercy. His smile is the smile of the Father's love. His tears are the tears of divine compassion. Every feature of His Face reveals the mystery of a God who chose to be known, not as an abstract idea, but as a living Friend.

The world today is hungry for this revelation. Faces surround us on every screen, yet they rarely reflect the peace and love for which the soul longs. Only one Face can satisfy the human heart. Only one countenance can restore the world's lost hope. That is the Face of Christ, radiant in the Eucharist, shining in the saints, and calling to each of us: *"Seek My Face."*

To begin this mission, then, is to make a resolution of the heart: that above all other desires, we will seek the Face of Christ. For in seeking Him, we shall find salvation.

MEDITATION 2

The Eucharist: Radiance of His Presence

When Philip said to Jesus, *"Lord, show us the Father, and we shall be satisfied"* (John 14:8), he voiced the cry of every human heart. Our Lord's reply was simple and stunning: *"He who has seen Me has seen the Father."* To see the Face of Christ is to behold the Father's love. And nowhere is that love more radiant, more tangible, than in the Eucharist.

The Eucharist is not merely a symbol or reminder. It is Christ Himself — Body, Blood, Soul, and Divinity — veiled under the appearance of bread and wine. Yet though veiled, He is not hidden. His Real Presence shines through to the eyes of faith. The Host may seem humble, but for those who adore Him, it is nothing less than the Face of Christ turned toward His people.

Archbishop Fulton J. **Sheen on**ce said that every Holy Hour is an hour spent "looking at Him and letting Him look at you." This is the essence of Eucharistic adoration: a meeting of gazes. We look upon the Host, and though we see only whiteness, our faith tells us that the Face of Christ is there — the same Face that once smiled upon the leper, wept over Jerusalem, and shone with glory at the Resurrection. In return, He looks upon us with eyes that know our hearts, that pierce through our sins, that radiate mercy.

To kneel before the tabernacle or monstrance is therefore to step into the light of His countenance. It is to allow His radiance to penetrate the shadows within us. Like the sun shining on a darkened room, His Eucharistic Presence illumines our souls, revealing both the dust of sin and the beauty of grace. We cannot remain unchanged when exposed to such light.

The world desperately needs this radiance. Surrounded by the artificial glow of screens, many souls grow dim with fatigue and despair. But Christ's Eucharistic light is not artificial; it is eternal. It restores, renews, and enkindles. To bring the world back to life, Catholics must once again be reflectors of that light, carrying it from the altar into every corner of society.

The Eucharist is therefore not only the radiance of Christ's presence — it is also the radiance of our mission. To adore Him is to be transformed by Him. To receive Him is to become like Him. To look upon His Face in the Host is to learn how to be His Face for others.

Let us then resolve to return often to the Eucharist. Let us spend time in the light of His Presence, until our lives, too, begin to glow with His love. For only those who have reflected His radiance can become, in Sheen's words, "Christ-bearers to the world."

MEDITATION 3

Reparation: Love's Response

Love, when it sees that it has wounded the Beloved, seeks to make amends. This is the essence of reparation. It is not a cold duty or grim obligation, but the spontaneous movement of a heart pierced by love. When we realize that our sins have struck the Face of Christ, bruised and spat upon, we cannot remain indifferent. Love compels us to console Him.

Archbishop Fulton J. Sheen often reminded us that sin is not merely the breaking of a law, but the wounding of a Person. Every sin is a turning away from the Face of Christ. Yet every act of reparation is a turning back, a way of saying, *"Lord, I am sorry. I love You. Let me share in Your sorrow so that I may share in Your joy."*

The saints understood this. St. Thérèse of Lisieux, who united her Little Way to the devotion of the Holy Face, longed to wipe away the tears of Jesus with her small sacrifices. St. Veronica, on the road to Calvary, braved the jeers of the crowd to press her veil to His blood-stained Face. Each act of reparation, great or small, becomes a caress upon the wounds of Christ.

Reparation is not confined to heroic deeds; it can be woven into the fabric of daily life. A hidden prayer offered for those who blaspheme, an act of patience in the face of provocation, an hour of adoration before the Eucharist — all these are ways of repairing for the coldness and ingratitude that Our Lord suffers. Every act of love is like a drop of balm upon His wounds.

Why is reparation needed? Because love demands it, and because souls depend on it. Sheen often compared reparation to standing in the breach: when sin threatens to overwhelm the world, the reparative soul intercedes, offering love where hatred abounds, light where darkness spreads. Reparation is participation in the very mission of Christ, who offered Himself as the ultimate act of love to heal the broken bond between God and man.

The Face of Christ, once disfigured by sin, now shines with the glory of forgiveness. To console Him in His suffering is to share in His triumph. And as we make reparation, we ourselves are transformed. Our hearts grow tender, our love more selfless, our gaze more fixed on His.

Let us then embrace reparation, not with fear, but with joy. For in repairing the wounds of Christ, we learn the deepest secret of love: that when we give Him our little acts of sorrow, He returns to us the radiance of His smile.

MEDITATION 4

The Light that Shines in Darkness

From the opening of St. John's Gospel, we hear the promise: *"The light shines in the darkness, and the darkness has not overcome it."* (John 1:5) Christ is that light. His Face is the radiance of God shining into the shadows of a fallen world. And yet, the mystery of our faith is that this light is revealed most powerfully in moments of suffering, trial, and apparent defeat.

Look to Calvary. The sky darkens, the earth trembles, and all seems lost. Yet in the midst of this darkness, the crucified Face of Christ shines with the brightest love. His eyes, though dimmed with blood, radiate forgiveness. His lips, parched with thirst, proclaim mercy. His countenance, marred beyond recognition, is at the same time the most radiant revelation of God's glory.

Archbishop Fulton J. Sheen often said that the Cross is like a blackboard upon which God wrote His deepest lesson: that love is stronger than hate, that life conquers death, that light is never extinguished by darkness. The Cross does not hide the Face of Christ; it reveals it.

Our world today knows much darkness. The shadow of unbelief, the weight of sin, the wounds of division and violence — all threaten to obscure hope. And yet, precisely in these moments, the light of Christ shines most clearly. Every soul that turns in faith to His Eucharistic Presence, every act of reparation, every prayer whispered in love — these are sparks of light piercing the night.

It is not only the great saints who bear this light. Every Christian, by baptism, is called to reflect the Face of Christ in a world desperate for hope. In the patient endurance of suffering, in the courage to forgive, in the quiet witness of prayer, the light of His countenance shines through us. As Sheen said, "The greatest contribution we can make to the world is to let Christ shine through us."

To live in the light of Christ's Face is therefore not to escape the world's darkness but to transform it. We carry His radiance not by fleeing from the Cross but by embracing it. In doing so, our own faces become illumined, so that even in trial, others may see in us a reflection of the One who said: *"I am the Light of the world. Whoever follows Me will not walk in darkness, but will have the light of life."* (John 8:12)

Let us then walk with confidence into the world's shadows, not with fear, but with the certainty that the light of Christ's Face shines through us. For the darker the night, the more brightly His countenance is revealed.

MEDITATION 5

The Mission of Evangelization

When Philip once cried, *"Lord, show us the Father, and we shall be satisfied"* (John 14:8), he expressed not only a personal longing but the desire of every soul. The Face of Christ is the answer to that desire. To contemplate Him in adoration is to be filled; to proclaim Him in mission is to share that fullness with the world. Evangelization, then, is nothing less than reflecting His Face so that others may see and believe.

Archbishop Fulton J. Sheen was above all a missionary. Whether speaking to millions on the radio, preaching in cathedrals, or visiting the poor, his one goal was to make the Face of Christ visible to the world. He often reminded us that people today listen not so much to arguments as to witnesses. The truest evangelist is the one whose life shines with the radiance of Christ's countenance.

This mission begins in silence before the Eucharist. To bring Christ to the world, we must first be transformed by gazing upon Him ourselves. Sheen would spend his Holy Hour each day not as preparation for preaching, but as communion with the Lord. Yet it was in that silence that the fire of his words was kindled. Evangelization flows from adoration. We cannot show the Face of Christ unless we have first sought it.

The world longs for this witness. In an age of masks, when faces are often hidden behind distractions, divisions, and despair, the Church is called to reveal the true Face of hope. Evangelization is not merely programs or strategies; it is the shining forth of Christ's love through lives that have been illumined by Him. Every Christian is a missionary. Every parish is a mission station. Every home can be a beacon of His light.

To evangelize is also to repair the image of God in souls disfigured by sin. Just as Veronica's veil bore the imprint of Christ's suffering Face, so our witness is meant to impress His image upon others. By words of truth, by deeds of mercy, by the patient endurance of trials, we leave behind the living imprint of His love.

The task may seem daunting, but Sheen would remind us that God needs only willing instruments. The world does not expect us to be brilliant; it expects us to be radiant. It does not require us to have all the answers; it longs to see in us the Face of Christ.

Let us then accept the mission of evangelization with courage. Let us gaze upon His Face in the Eucharist until our own faces are transfigured with His light. And then, like Moses descending from the mountain, let us go forth so that all who meet us may see reflected, however dimly, the radiance of the One who saves.

MEDITATION 6

Mary, Mirror of the Face of Christ

When a child is born, those who gather around the crib often remark: *"He has his mother's eyes… her smile… her face."* In the mystery of the Incarnation, it was the opposite that was true. The Face of Christ bore the likeness of His Mother. The eternal Word took flesh from Mary, and the human features that revealed the invisible God were fashioned in her womb.

Mary is therefore the first and most perfect mirror of the Face of Christ. To look upon her is to see the reflection of her Son; to draw near to her is to be led unfailingly to Him. As Archbishop Fulton J. Sheen often said, *"Never do we honour Mary more than when we speak of her as pointing the way to her Son."*

At Bethlehem, she gazed with love upon His newborn Face. At Nazareth, she saw the smile of God in the boy who was her Child and her Lord. On Calvary, her eyes met His eyes as His countenance was disfigured by suffering. Through it all, she remained faithful, holding in her heart the vision of His Face even when it was hidden from the world.

Mary also reflects Christ's light to us. Just as the moon has no light of its own but shines with the radiance of the sun, so Mary's beauty comes entirely from her union with her Son. She is the "Woman clothed with the sun" (Revelation 12:1), whose very being magnifies the Lord. When we see her tenderness, we glimpse the mercy of Christ.

When we behold her purity, we perceive the holiness of Christ. When we experience her intercession, we feel the compassion of Christ.

This is why devotion to Mary is never a distraction but always a safeguard of true faith. She magnifies Christ. She teaches us how to gaze upon His Face with love, how to endure suffering with Him, how to reflect His light in a dark world. Every genuine Marian devotion is a pathway to deeper contemplation of Christ.

For this reason, reparation to the Holy Face is inseparable from devotion to the Sorrowful Mother. Just as she once wiped the blood from His countenance on the road to Calvary through Veronica's veil, so now she teaches us to console Him with our prayers and sacrifices. She is the first disciple of the Holy Face, and she continues to form us as her children in this school of love.

Let us then turn to Mary with confidence. In her, we will see reflected the very Face we long to behold. And as we walk with her, she will gently teach us to become mirrors ourselves — reflecting Christ to others until the whole world is illumined with His light.

MEDITATION 7

The Cross and the
Glory of His Face

The Gospels tell us that as Christ hung upon the Cross, *"there was darkness over the whole land"* (Matthew 27:45). To the world, it appeared that His Face was disfigured, His mission defeated, His light extinguished. Yet for those with eyes of faith, this was not defeat but triumph. The Cross is the throne from which Christ reigns, and His marred countenance is the very revelation of God's glory.

Archbishop Fulton J. Sheen often said that the world's idea of glory is power, prestige, and success. God's idea of glory is sacrifice, humility, and love. On Calvary, Christ's Face — bruised, spit upon, crowned with thorns — revealed a beauty the world had never seen: the beauty of love willing to suffer for the beloved. This is the glory of the Cross.

The prophet Isaiah foresaw it: *"He had no form or comeliness that we should look at Him, and no beauty that we should desire Him"* (Isaiah 53:2). Yet hidden beneath the bruises was the splendour of divine mercy. What appeared to be ugliness was in truth the most radiant beauty, for it was the beauty of a God who loves without measure.

At Calvary, Mary's eyes met the eyes of her Son. In that exchange of sorrow and love, the glory of the Cross was already beginning to shine. Mary did not look away from the disfigured Face of Christ; she adored it. So too must we. The world flees from suffering, but the Christian sees in it the very place where God's glory is revealed.

This mystery transforms our own crosses. When trials mar the "face" of our lives, when suffering leaves us scarred, we are tempted to believe that God has abandoned us. But it is precisely then that His glory can shine through us most powerfully. For every act of patient endurance, every offering of sorrow united to His, becomes a reflection of the beauty of the Crucified Face.

The Cross, then, is not the eclipse of God's glory but its revelation. It teaches us that true beauty is sacrificial love, and true victory is found in surrender. When we look upon a crucifix, we see not merely a man condemned but God enthroned. His crown of thorns is His crown of majesty; His broken Face is the radiant icon of divine mercy.

Let us therefore not turn away from the Cross. Let us gaze upon the glory of His Face, even when it is marred by suffering. For there we will learn the deepest truth: that every wound borne in love becomes radiant, every tear shed in faith becomes luminous, and every cross embraced with Christ becomes a share in His eternal glory.

MEDITATION 8

The Church: His Face in the World

When Christ ascended into heaven, His visible presence was withdrawn. Yet He did not leave the world without His Face. He entrusted His presence to the Church, which is His Body, His Bride, and His visible sign in history. Through the Church, Christ continues to look upon the world with eyes of mercy, to speak with words of truth, and to shine with the radiance of His countenance.

Archbishop Fulton J. Sheen loved to call the Church "Christ prolonging Himself in time and space." To encounter the Church is to encounter Christ — sometimes through her sacraments, sometimes through her teaching, sometimes through the simple witness of ordinary believers. Though imperfect in her human members, the Church remains the sacrament of Christ's Face to the nations.

The Eucharist is the most radiant expression of this mystery. Every Mass is a moment when Christ once again shows His Face to the world, hidden yet real, veiled yet radiant. But the Church also reveals His countenance through her works of mercy. When the hungry are fed, the sick visited, the poor uplifted, the forgotten consoled, the world glimpses the compassion etched upon His Face.

Fulton Sheen often reminded us that the greatest scandal in the Church is not her weakness but her failure to reflect Christ. When Christians become disfigured by pride, division, or sin, the world turns away in disappointment, for it does not see the Face it longs to see. But when Christians live with humility, charity, and joy, even the most skeptical hearts can be won.

This is why every believer shares responsibility for the Church's witness. We are each called to be the "face" of Christ in our homes, our parishes, our workplaces. In our patience, people must see His patience; in our forgiveness, His mercy; in our love, His love. As St. Teresa of Avila once wrote: *"Christ has no body now but yours, no hands, no feet on earth but yours."* In the same way, we might say: Christ has no visible Face now but yours.

To belong to the Church is therefore not merely to carry a name but to carry a mission: to let Christ's countenance shine through us so clearly that others may recognize Him. In an age darkened by confusion and division, the world needs once again to see the luminous unity of Christ's Body, the serene beauty of His Bride, and the radiant witness of His saints.

Let us not be ashamed, then, of our identity as members of His Church. Let us show the world the true Face of Christ — in the sacraments we celebrate, in the love we live, and in the hope we proclaim. For when the Church reflects His countenance, the world sees not merely an institution, but the living Face of the Saviour.

MEDITATION 9

Transformation Through Contemplation

To gaze upon the Face of Christ is not a passive act. It is an encounter that changes us. Just as Moses descended Mount Sinai with his face shining after speaking with God, so too the Christian who spends time before the Eucharist carries away the radiance of that divine encounter.

Archbishop Fulton J. Sheen called this the "Law of Transformation." In his words, *"We become like those with whom we associate, and if we associate with Christ in the Blessed Sacrament, we will become like Him."* This is the secret of contemplation: by fixing our eyes on Him, we slowly begin to reflect what we see.

The world often tells us that to be transformed we must strive harder, achieve more, or reinvent ourselves. But true transformation does not come from self-improvement; it comes from self-surrender. The soul that kneels quietly before the tabernacle, day after day, is silently remade. Pride gives way to humility, fear to trust, selfishness to love. Without fanfare or noise, the countenance of Christ begins to shine through the believer.

This is why Eucharistic adoration is not optional for those who wish to live as Christ's witnesses. Evangelization, reparation, mission — all of these are hollow if they are not rooted in the slow, patient work of contemplation. To be Christ's Face in the world, we must first allow His gaze to penetrate us, heal us, and make us new.

The saints bear witness to this transformation. St. Thérèse, gazing upon the crucifix, discovered her Little Way of trust. St. John Vianney, lost in hours of adoration, radiated holiness to his parish. Fulton Sheen himself, faithful to his daily Holy Hour, was able to carry the light of Christ to millions. Their secret was not genius, strategy, or strength. It was simply this: they allowed themselves to be transformed by contemplating His Face.

And this transformation is not for saints alone. Every soul who prays before the Blessed Sacrament enters into the same school of love. Christ does not ask for eloquence or achievement; He asks only for our presence. As we sit in silence, He works in us. As we remain faithful, He reshapes us. As we look upon Him, He makes His Face shine within us.

This is the destiny of every Christian: not merely to admire Christ from afar, but to become His living image. The world is waiting for such souls — men and women whose faces bear the quiet glow of one who has been with the Lord.

Let us then commit ourselves to contemplation. Let us take time each day to seek His Face, not rushing, not demanding, but resting in His presence. For those who contemplate His countenance will themselves be transformed into His likeness, until at last we shall see Him face to Face in glory.

MEDITATION 10

Lord, Show Us Thy Face and We Shall Be Saved

The ancient cry of Israel has become the cry of the Church: *"Lord, show us Thy Face, and we shall be saved."* (Psalm 80:3) This longing echoes through every page of Scripture, every devotion of the saints, and every hour spent before the tabernacle. It is the cry of the human heart — to see God, to be seen by Him, and to live in the light of His countenance.

In Jesus Christ, this cry has been answered. The Face of the invisible God has been revealed in the Word made flesh. That Face was radiant in Bethlehem, sorrowful on Calvary, glorious in the Resurrection, and now hidden yet present in the Eucharist. To look upon His countenance is to see mercy incarnate, love victorious, hope fulfilled.

Archbishop Fulton J. Sheen taught that the mission of every Christian is to bear this Face to the world. We are not merely disciples but reflectors. Like the moon reflecting the sun, our task is to shine with a light not our own, so that all who look upon us may glimpse the radiance of Christ. Our families, our parishes, our workplaces, our communities — all are waiting for such light.

This mission is not complicated. It begins in adoration. It deepens through reparation. It grows in the silence of contemplation. And it overflows in evangelization, as we bring Christ's love to a world longing for His presence. To seek His Face is to be sent with His Face

— to let others encounter Him in our gaze, our words, our actions, and our love.

The journey has brought us here: to the simple but profound truth that salvation is found in the shining of His countenance. And this is not only a hope for the future but a reality for today. Every time we kneel before the Eucharist, every time we whisper a prayer of reparation, every time we show mercy to another, His Face is revealed anew.

One day, this longing will be satisfied in full. The veil will be lifted, and we shall see Him as He is — no longer hidden, no longer in mystery, but face to Face in eternal glory. Until then, we walk by faith, seeking His presence in the Eucharist, in the poor, in the Church, and in one another.

Let us then take up the mission entrusted to us. Let us echo with confidence the cry of the saints, the cry of the Church, the cry of every longing soul:

"Lord, show us Thy Face, and we shall be saved."

Fulton Sheen on the Eucharist and Adoration

Part One:
Sheen's Core Themes on the Eucharist

Archbishop Fulton J. Sheen's life was marked by one unbroken devotion: his daily Holy Hour before the Blessed Sacrament. For over sixty years, he kept this appointment with Christ, no matter how busy his schedule or demanding his ministry. In that silent hour, Sheen found the secret of his strength, the fire of his preaching, and the light of his wisdom.

Fulton Sheen insisted that the Eucharist is not a thing but a Person — the living Christ, present in Body, Blood, Soul, and Divinity. To kneel before the tabernacle is to look into the eyes of Jesus, hidden yet radiant. He often said that the greatest tragedy of the modern Church was not persecution but neglect of this Presence. The cure for a weary world, he believed, was a return to the altar — a return to gazing upon the Face of Christ in the Host.

For Fulton Sheen, the Holy Hour was not simply about speaking but about being seen. He encouraged souls to spend time before the Eucharist as lovers spend time together: in silence, in presence, in communion of hearts. "We become like those we love," he taught. "If we love the Eucharist, we will become like Him whom we adore."

Part Two:
A Treasury of Sheen's Words

- *"The greatest love story of all time is contained in a tiny white Host."*

- *"The Holy Hour is a privileged time to grow more into His likeness. We become like those with whom we associate. If we spend time with Christ, we will become like Christ."*

- *"The only reason for doing a Holy Hour is to grow more and more into His likeness. We come not so much to talk as to be looked at by Him."*

- *"As the sun is never diminished by shining on one flower or a million, so Christ's Presence in the Eucharist is never divided. He is fully present to you as if you were the only one in the world."*

- *"When we make a Holy Hour, we are not alone with Christ. The whole Church is present with us, because the Church lives from the Eucharist."*

- *"If we wish to know the Face of Christ, we will find it in the tabernacle. Hidden there, He waits, radiant with love."*

- *"When we are before the Blessed Sacrament, let us open our hearts. Our Lord speaks to us far more in silence than we can ever speak to Him."*

- *"The purpose of the Holy Hour is not to change God, but to change ourselves. We need the Holy Hour as a compass to keep us on the right path."*

- *"The Holy Hour is like an oxygen tank to revive the breath of the Holy Spirit in the midst of the polluted atmosphere of the world."*

- *"If you do not worship God, you will worship something else. The Eucharist is where true worship is restored."*

- *"In the Holy Hour we are not alone with Jesus; we are with the whole Church, adoring Him on behalf of those who do not."*

- *"The greatest love we can show to others is to bring them into the presence of the Eucharist."*

Part Three:
Praying with Sheen before the Eucharist

Themes for Reflection

1. **Presence** – Christ is not a memory, but truly present in the Eucharist.

   Kneel quietly before the tabernacle or monstrance. Begin with Sheen's prayer:

   "Lord Jesus, I believe You are truly present in the Eucharist.
   I adore You, I love You, and I trust in You."

2. **Silence** – God's deepest words are spoken in silence; adoration trains the soul to listen.

   Spend several minutes in silence, letting one of Sheen's quotations echo in your heart. For example:

   "The greatest love story of all time is
   contained in a tiny white Host."

3. **Reparation** – Every Holy Hour consoles the Heart and Face of Christ for those who ignore or reject Him.

   Offer your Holy Hour for those who do not believe, do not adore, do not love Him.

   Pray: *"O Lord, let the light of Your Face shine upon all souls, especially those who are far from You."*

4. **Transformation** – In adoration, we become like the One we behold; His Face is imprinted upon our souls.

Close with Sheen's reminder: *"The purpose of the Holy Hour is not to change God, but to change ourselves."*

Ask Christ to imprint His countenance upon your life, so that you may reflect Him to others.

5. **Mission** – The fire of evangelization is kindled before the Eucharist; adoration always sends us out renewed.

Prayers for Reflection

1. Adoration:

"Lord, You are here, fully present in this Host. I gaze upon You, and I allow You to gaze upon me."

O Jesus, truly present in the Most Holy Sacrament of the Altar, I adore You with all the love of my heart. Hidden under the veil of bread, You are the same Lord who walked among us, who suffered for us, and who rose in glory. I gaze upon You, and I let You gaze upon me. May this hour in Your presence bring light to my soul and peace to the world.

2. Reparation:

"I console Your wounded Face, Lord, for every neglect and every indifference toward Your Eucharistic Presence."

Lord Jesus, I come before Your Eucharistic Face to console You for the coldness, neglect, and ingratitude You suffer in this Sacrament of love. I unite myself to the sorrows of Your Sacred Heart and to the tears of Your Blessed Mother. Receive my prayers, my sacrifices, and my love as a small act of reparation, and through them, draw many souls back to Your merciful Heart.

3. Transformation:

"Let this time with You make me more like You. Shine upon me until Your Face is reflected in mine."

4. Mission:

"Send me forth as Your witness, Lord. May all who see me today see in me the reflection of Your Eucharistic Face."

5. Prayer for Priests

Eternal High Priest, Jesus Christ, I adore You in the Sacrament of the Altar and I intercede for all Your priests. Sanctify them, protect them, and fill them with the fire of Your love. May they be faithful to their daily Holy Hour, fervent in their ministry, and shining witnesses of Your Eucharistic Face to the world.

6. Prayer for the Conversion of Sinners

Merciful Jesus, by the light of Your Eucharistic Face, draw back to You all who wander in darkness. Heal wounded hearts, forgive sinners, and renew the world by the power of Your love. For their sake, I offer this hour in union with Your sacrifice on the Cross.

7. Prayer of Thanksgiving

Thank You, Lord, for this time with You. Thank You for the gift of the Eucharist, for the grace of Your mercy, and for the light of Your countenance. As I leave this holy place, may Your Face shine within me, so that others may see Your love reflected in my life. Amen.

Guide to a Holy Hour
of Eucharistic Reparation

Why Make a Holy Hour?

Archbishop Fulton J. Sheen often said: *"The Holy Hour is the hour that makes my day. Without it, I would not be able to preach Christ."* For sixty years, he spent one hour each day before the Blessed Sacrament, in silence, adoration, and reparation. He knew that the Church's greatest need was not more activity, but more intimacy with Christ in the Eucharist.

The Holy Hour is a time to be with Jesus, to gaze upon His Eucharistic Face, and to let Him gaze upon you. It is a time to console Him for the coldness, indifference, and ingratitude He suffers in the Sacrament of His love. It is also the time when He heals, strengthens, and transforms the soul.

How to Structure a Holy Hour

1. Preparation (5 minutes)

- Begin in silence. Make the Sign of the Cross slowly.

- Offer a short prayer of presence:

- *"Lord, I am here. You are here. Let this time be Yours."*

2. Adoration (15 minutes)

- Gaze upon the Host in silence. Allow the words of Scripture to stir your heart:

- *"Be still, and know that I am God."* (Psalm 46:10)

- Pray slowly: *"Lord, show me Your Face."*

3. Reparation (15 minutes)

- Offer prayers for sins against the Eucharist and against the Holy Face.

- Pray the Act of Reparation

- Unite your sorrows with the sorrows of Mary and Veronica, who consoled the suffering Face of Christ.

4. Intercession (10 minutes)

- Pray for family, friends, the Church, and the world.

- Offer special prayers for priests and for the conversion of sinners — Sheen's daily intention.

- Use Sheen's aspiration: *"Eternal Father, I offer You the Body, Blood, Soul, and Divinity of Your Son, truly present in the Eucharist, for the reparation of sins."*

5. Thanksgiving (10 minutes)

- Thank Jesus for His Presence, His mercy, and His love.

- Pray an Our Father, Hail Mary, and Glory Be slowly.

- Conclude with - *"Sacred Face of Jesus, may Your light shine upon me, upon the Church, and upon the whole world."*

6. Closing (5 minutes)

- Sit briefly in silence.

- Make the Sign of the Cross.

- Leave the chapel quietly, carrying His Presence into your day.

Tips for Making a Holy Hour

- **Be faithful, not perfect.** Don't worry about distractions; simply return your gaze to Him.

- **Use Scripture.** Read slowly from the Gospels or Psalms, especially passages on the Face of Christ.

- **Bring a prayer book.** Use the prayers in this volume when words fail.

- **Offer your hour.** Intend it for reparation, for priests, for sinners, for the needs of the world.

- **Be present.** More than anything, give Him your time and your heart.

Prayer to Begin a Holy Hour

Lord Jesus, I come before You in the Sacrament of Your love. I adore You, I thank You, and I desire to console You. Receive this hour as a small act of reparation for my sins and for the sins of the world. Shine upon me with the light of Your Face, and make me a faithful witness of Your love.
Amen.

CONCLUDING WORD

Sent from the Light
of His Countenance

T o gaze upon the Face of Christ is not only to contemplate a mystery of faith but to encounter a living Presence. The Holy Face is not confined to an image or a memory; it shines forth most radiantly in the Eucharist, where Christ veils His glory under the humble appearances of bread and wine. Before the tabernacle or in the silence of adoration, the promise is fulfilled: we behold God face to Face.

Archbishop Fulton J. Sheen reminds us that every Holy Hour is a privileged moment when heaven bends low to earth, when the divine countenance gazes back at us with love. In the Eucharist, the bruised and glorified Face of Jesus looks upon us, inviting our hearts to be transformed.

As this book closes, let it open into worship. Kneel before the Eucharistic Lord, and pray with the Church: *"Lord, show us Thy Face, and we shall be saved."* May His Eucharistic radiance light our path in this life, and lead us one day to the unveiled vision of His glory for all eternity.

PART V

OVERCOMING SIN, PRACTICING VIRTUE, AND LIVING THE BEATITUDES

OVERCOMING SIN, PRACTICING VIRTUE, AND LIVING THE BEATITUDES

Meditations with Fulton J. Sheen
A Mission of Interior Renewal and Divine Transformation

T he spiritual life is a battlefield of the heart — a place where grace and weakness meet, and where the soul learns the art of surrender. Archbishop Fulton J. Sheen reminds us that sanctity is not the absence of struggle, but the perfection of love in the midst of it. Each virtue conquered, each sin overcome, and each Beatitude embraced becomes a step toward the likeness of Christ.

Description:

In these meditations, we walk with the Master who taught on the Mount and died on the Cross — the same Christ who now calls us to be poor in spirit, pure in heart, merciful, and steadfast in love. Here we discover that holiness is not a distant ideal but a lived reality — forged through daily fidelity, transformed by grace, and crowned in charity.

This section of the Sheen Mission Series is an invitation to interior renewal — to confront the seven sins that darken the soul, to practice the seven virtues that perfect it, and to live the Beatitudes that unite us to the heart of the Saviour.

"The Beatitudes are the eight pillars upon which the Kingdom of God is built. To live them is to live the life of Christ Himself."

— Archbishop Fulton J. Sheen

PREFACE

Overcoming Sin, Practicing Virtue, and Living the Beatitudes

Introduction

The Seven Last Words of Christ are more than a record of what Christ said before dying. They are the living voice of God addressing every generation, every heart, and every struggle. Archbishop Fulton J. Sheen returned again and again to these words throughout his preaching, because he recognized in them the perfect summary of the Christian life.

Archbishop Fulton J. Sheen said: *"Unless souls are saved, nothing is saved."* The Cross was His mission of salvation; our share in it is to let grace transform us into saints.

In three of his classic works — *Victory over Vice*, *The Seven Virtues*, and *The Cross and the Beatitudes* — Sheen showed how each Word of the Crucified Christ provides a remedy for sin, a lesson in virtue, and a living portrait of the Beatitudes. At Calvary, Christ not only saves us; He also shows us how to live.

What follows is a synthesis of Sheen's insights. It is a spiritual roadmap: first, how to **overcome sin**; second, how to **practice virtue**; and third, how to **live the Beatitudes**.

Overcoming Sin

At the Cross, sin is unmasked and defeated. Pride is conquered by humility, anger by forgiveness, lust by purity, envy by gratitude, sloth by perseverance, greed by generosity, gluttony by fasting and self-denial. Each vice finds its antidote in the Passion of Christ.

Sheen's Insight:

"Our Lord did not die to remove suffering, but to give meaning to it. Each word from the Cross not only redeems but also heals the wounds sin has left in us."

Sheen's Wisdom:

"The Cross is not an accident in life, but the answer to sin. Each word from Calvary is a medicine — bitter perhaps, but healing for the soul."

Practicing Virtue

Every virtue is a share in the life of Christ:

- **Fortitude** endures trials with patience.

- **Hope** looks to Paradise, as the Good Thief did.

- **Prudence** chooses rightly in the light of the Cross.

- **Faith** clings to God in darkness, as He did in His cry of abandonment.

- **Temperance** disciplines desire.

- **Justice** gives to God and neighbor what is their due.

- **Charity** forgives, thirsts, and loves without limit.

Sheen's Insight:

"Virtue is not mere avoidance of sin, but the blossoming of love. At Calvary, Christ shows us that the highest virtue is to give oneself completely."

Sheen's Wisdom:

"Virtue is not repression but transformation. Calvary shows us not what to avoid, but what to become."

Living the Beatitudes

The Beatitudes are not lofty ideals but the very shape of Calvary:

- Meekness: His silence before accusers.

- Mercy: His forgiveness of His enemies.

- Purity of heart: His undivided will to the Father.

- Poor in spirit: Christ who emptied Himself.

- Hunger for righteousness: His thirst for souls.

- Peacemaking: His reconciling of Heaven and earth.

- Mourning: Mary and the faithful who grieved with Him.

- Persecution for righteousness: His Cross itself.

To live the Beatitudes is to live beneath the Cross — humble, meek, merciful, pure, steadfast, and faithful unto death.

Sheen's Insight:

"The Beatitudes are Christ's autobiography. On the Cross, they are not preached but lived."

"The Beatitudes are not ideals to admire but laws to live. On Calvary, they are not preached but practiced."

Conclusion

The Cross is not only our redemption but our pattern of life. Practicing virtue, overcoming sin, and living the Beatitudes are the fruits of Calvary. They are the way we turn meditation into action, prayer into witness, and faith into love.

At the Cross, Christ conquers sin, perfects virtue, and embodies the Beatitudes. His Seven Last Words are not only His farewell gift to the world, but also a practical guide for our sanctification.

To stand beneath the Cross is to enter the school of Christ. Here we learn how to overcome vice, how to practice virtue, and how to live the Beatitudes — not in theory, but in the flesh, in daily life, in love poured out.

As Archbishop Sheen said: *"The Cross is not something to be escaped; it is something to be embraced. It is the key, not only to heaven, but to happiness here on earth."*

Introduction to Reflections on Overcoming Sin, Practicing Virtue, and Living the Beatitudes

T he meditations you have just read invite you to stand at Calvary, listening to the Seven Last Words of Christ and discovering their power for the Christian soul. These final reflections, gathered here as an appendix, continue that same pilgrimage — but with a shift of focus.

Here we move from the mystery of the Cross itself to its practical fruit in daily life: overcoming sin, cultivating virtue, and embracing the Beatitudes. Archbishop Fulton Sheen often reminded us that the Passion of Christ is not merely to be admired but to be imitated. To gaze upon the Crucified is to be invited into conversion, renewal, and holiness.

This section is placed at the end of the book deliberately. Not all readers may feel ready to take up these demanding meditations right away. They are offered as a companion guide for those who wish to go further, who wish to let the Cross shape not only their prayer but their way of living.

Whether read immediately or returned to later, these reflections are meant to be a **practical school of discipleship**, showing how the victory of Calvary takes root in our own lives.

PART I

Overcoming Sin

Introduction

Before we can live fully in the grace of the Cross, we must first face the reality of sin. Archbishop Fulton Sheen often reminded us that sin is not simply the breaking of a law but the wounding of love — the rejection of God's friendship. At Calvary, Christ bore every sin in His own Body so that we might be free.

These reflections are not meant to discourage, but to liberate. By naming the sins that so often enslave the human heart, we can learn to place them beneath the Cross and discover there the mercy that heals and restores.

- Reflection 1 – Overcoming the Sin of Anger

- Reflection 2 – Overcoming the Sin of Envy

- Reflection 3 – Overcoming the Sin of Lust

- Reflection 4 – Overcoming the Sin of Pride

- Reflection 5 – Overcoming the Sin of Gluttony

- Reflection 6 – Overcoming the Sin of Sloth

- Reflection 7 – Overcoming the Sin of Greed

REFLECTION 1

Overcoming the Sin of Anger

The First Word: *"Father, forgive them, for they know not what they do."*

Reflection – Anger Healed by Forgiveness

Anger burns hot when we feel wronged, betrayed, or humiliated. It demands vengeance, clings to resentment, and refuses peace. Yet the Cross reveals a new path: when Jesus was mocked, scourged, and crucified, He did not curse His enemies — He forgave them.

The true antidote to anger is not suppression, but transformation. In forgiving, Christ shows us that anger is conquered by mercy.

Sheen on Anger in the First Word

> *"Anger is love of justice perverted to revenge. Our Lord satisfied justice not by punishing, but by forgiving. The cure for anger is forgiveness — not once, but seventy times seven."*

Archbishop Sheen taught that anger wastes its fire on destruction, while Christ's fire of love transforms pain into peace.

Illustration – The Power of Forgiveness

A man whose son was killed by violence stunned the courtroom by telling the offender: *"I forgive you. I will pray for you."* That act broke the cycle of hate. His courage revealed that forgiveness disarms anger more powerfully than retaliation ever could.

Invitation – Letting Go of Wrath

To overcome anger, we must release our claim to vengeance and hand it over to God. Forgiveness does not mean forgetting the wrong, but choosing not to let anger rule our hearts.

Ask yourself:

- *Do I allow anger to poison my thoughts and words?*

- *Who is God asking me to forgive today?*

- *Am I willing to surrender my anger to the Cross, where love has the last word?*

Closing Prayer

Lord Jesus, You answered anger with forgiveness. Take from me the poison of wrath, the chains of resentment, and the desire for revenge. Teach me to forgive as You forgave, so that anger may give way to peace. **Amen.**

REFLECTION 2

Overcoming the Sin of Envy

The Second Word: *"This day you will be with Me in Paradise."*

Reflection – Envy Healed by Trust in Mercy

Envy looks at the blessings of others with resentment, as if God's generosity to them were an injustice to us. At Calvary, two thieves hung beside Jesus. One mocked Him, resentful even in death; the other humbled himself, asking only to be remembered.

In a single moment, envy was conquered by trust. The good thief discovered that God's mercy is never diminished by being shared — there is room in paradise for all.

Sheen on Envy in the Second Word

> *"Envy is sadness at another's good. The cure is to fix our eyes not on what others receive, but on Christ. One thief looked at Jesus with envy, the other with hope — and one was lost, the other saved."*

Archbishop Sheen showed that envy shrivels the soul, while gratitude and trust in mercy open it wide to heaven.

Illustration – The Joy of Another's Blessing

A young woman unable to conceive struggled with jealousy of her sister, who had children. At last, she began to pray not for her own blessing, but for joy in her sister's gift. To her surprise, peace entered her heart. Her envy gave way to gratitude, and she discovered freedom in celebrating another's good.

Invitation – Rejoicing in God's Generosity

To overcome envy, we must see life as gift. God's mercy is abundant, not scarce. The blessings of others are not threats, but reminders that God is generous to all.

Ask yourself:

- *Do I resent the blessings others receive?*

- *Can I learn to thank God for gifts He gives to my neighbor?*

- *Am I able to trust that He has a place in paradise prepared also for me?*

Closing Prayer

Lord Jesus,
You promised paradise to the repentant thief.
Take envy from my heart,
and teach me to rejoice in the good of others.
Help me to trust in Your mercy,
confident that Your blessings are without limit.
Amen.

REFLECTION 3

Overcoming the Sin of Lust

The Third Word: *"Behold your Mother."*

Reflection – Lust Healed by Purity of Love

Lust is the distortion of love into self-gratification, seeking pleasure without sacrifice. At Calvary, Jesus revealed the opposite: love that gives, not takes. In entrusting Mary to John and John to Mary, Christ established a new family of pure, selfless love.

The remedy to lust is not repression but transformation — learning to love with reverence, purity, and responsibility.

Sheen on Lust in the Third Word

> *"Lust looks upon others as objects; Christ looked upon His Mother and John as souls. Lust takes; love gives. Purity is not the absence of passion but the right ordering of it toward sacrifice."*

Archbishop Sheen taught that true purity is not weakness but strength: the discipline that makes love self-giving rather than self-seeking.

Illustration – Chastity as Love's Strength

A young couple once decided to live chastely before marriage. They admitted it was difficult but later said: *"Our love was purified by sacrifice. We gave each other respect before we gave our bodies."* Their story shows how purity prepares the heart for enduring love.

Invitation – Seeing with Pure Eyes

To overcome lust, we must see every person as Christ sees them — not as objects of desire but as children of God. Purity frees the heart to love rightly and deeply.

Ask yourself:

- *Do I treat others as objects of pleasure or as persons to be cherished?*

- *Am I willing to sacrifice comfort for purity of heart?*

- *Do I invite Mary, Mother most pure, into my struggles against lust?*

Closing Prayer

Lord Jesus, on the Cross You gave us Your Mother. Through her intercession, purify my heart and heal my desires. Teach me to love with reverence, to see others with pure eyes, and to make my life a gift of love. **Amen.**

REFLECTION 4

Overcoming the Sin of Pride

The Fourth Word: *"My God, My God, why have You forsaken Me?"*

Reflection – Pride Healed by Humble Faith

Pride is the root of all sin — the refusal to depend on God, the illusion that we are self-sufficient. On Calvary, Jesus embraced the very opposite: in His cry of abandonment, He showed total dependence on the Father, even when He felt nothing but silence.

The cure for pride is humility — admitting our weakness and trusting God even when we do not understand.

Sheen on Pride in the Fourth Word

> *"Pride says, 'I will not serve.' On the Cross, Christ showed the humility of the obedient Son. His cry was not despair but faith, clinging to the Father when the Father seemed absent."*

Archbishop Sheen explained that Christ dismantled pride by embracing radical humility — obedience unto death.

Illustration – Humility in Trial

A successful businessman lost everything in an economic collapse. At first, pride raged: *"How could this happen to me?"* Yet, slowly, he learned to pray: *"Into Your hands, Lord."* In losing his pride, he discovered deeper trust in God's providence.

Invitation – Living Humility

To overcome pride, we must embrace dependence on God, acknowledging that every breath is His gift. Humility is not weakness but strength: the courage to let God be God.

Ask yourself:

- *Do I rely on myself more than on God?*

- *Am I willing to surrender my pride and accept my dependence on Him?*

- *How can I grow in humility through obedience, patience, and trust?*

Closing Prayer

My God, when pride tempts me to rely on myself, teach me humility. When You seem silent, grant me faith to cling to You still. May I never exalt myself, but always find strength in surrender. **Amen.**

REFLECTION 5

Overcoming the Sin of Gluttony

The Fifth Word: *"I thirst."*

Reflection – Gluttony Healed by Holy Desire

Gluttony is the disordered craving for pleasure, especially in food and drink, but also in anything that dulls the soul with excess. On the Cross, Jesus revealed the deepest hunger and thirst of the human heart: not for excess, but for God.

His cry, *"I thirst,"* was more than physical. It was a thirst for righteousness, for souls, for the Father's will. Gluttony enslaves; holy desire frees.

Sheen on Gluttony in the Fifth Word

> *"When Our Lord said, 'I thirst,' He lifted desire to its highest level. Gluttony makes the stomach a god; Christ makes God our only satisfaction. The cure for gluttony is to hunger and thirst for justice."*

Archbishop Sheen emphasized that Jesus teaches us to redirect our appetites — from indulgence to sacrifice, from excess to holiness.

Illustration – Choosing the Higher Hunger

During Lent, a young man gave up alcohol, not just to deny himself but to replace the craving with prayer. He discovered that every time he resisted, his heart grew freer. His small sacrifice reminded him of Christ's thirst for souls.

Invitation – Purifying My Appetites

To overcome gluttony, we must discipline our desires, moderating what is good and rejecting what enslaves. True satisfaction is not in abundance but in God alone.

Ask yourself:

- *Do I allow food, drink, or comfort to master me?*

- *Am I willing to fast or sacrifice to discipline my appetites?*

- *Do I thirst more for pleasure or for God's love?*

Closing Prayer

O Jesus, who thirsted for souls upon the Cross, purify my desires. Teach me to hunger for righteousness, to thirst for holiness, and to find my true satisfaction in You alone. **Amen.**

REFLECTION 6

Overcoming the Sin of Sloth

The Sixth Word: *"It is finished."*

Reflection – Sloth Healed by Perseverance

Sloth is more than laziness; it is the refusal of effort in the spiritual life, the indifference to love's demands. On Calvary, Jesus declared: *"It is finished."* He did not abandon His mission halfway, but completed it in perfect fidelity.

Sloth withers the soul by keeping it lukewarm. The Cross ignites zeal by showing that love perseveres until the end.

Sheen on Sloth in the Sixth Word

> *"Sloth is not the love of ease, but the refusal of sacrifice. It is the sadness of the soul that will not strive for the highest. Our Lord conquered sloth by completing the work the Father gave Him to do."*

Archbishop Sheen taught that Christ's triumph over sloth calls us to wholehearted dedication in the duties of our state in life.

Illustration – Perseverance in Duty

A nurse caring for the dying once admitted: *"There are days I want to quit. But then I look at the crucifix and remember: He finished His work. I must finish mine."* Her fidelity transformed her weariness into love.

Invitation – Finishing the Work Entrusted to Me

To overcome sloth, we must embrace diligence in prayer, work, and love. Even small duties become holy when done with perseverance.

Ask yourself:

- *Am I neglecting prayer or duty out of laziness or indifference?*

- *Do I abandon commitments when they grow difficult?*

- *How can I persevere like Christ, completing the tasks given to me?*

Closing Prayer

Lord Jesus, You conquered sloth by finishing the work of redemption. Grant me zeal in prayer, diligence in duty, and perseverance in love. Let me not grow weary, but bring to completion the mission You entrust to me. **Amen.**

REFLECTION 7

Overcoming the Sin of Greed

The Seventh Word: *"Father, into Your hands I commend My spirit."*

Reflection – Greed Healed by Surrender

Greed clings tightly to possessions, power, and control, seeking security in what cannot last. On the Cross, Jesus did the opposite: He let go of everything — His strength, His breath, His very life — and placed it all into the Father's hands.

The cure for greed is generosity: surrendering our lives, goods, and hearts into God's keeping. Only when we let go do we discover true freedom.

Sheen on Greed in the Seventh Word

"Greed seeks to grasp; Christ chose to give. Greed hoards; Christ surrendered. In His final word, He placed everything in the Father's hands — teaching us that the only wealth worth keeping is the wealth of love."

Archbishop Sheen explained that greed shrinks the soul, but surrender expands it into eternity.

Illustration – Letting Go in Faith

A wealthy man once sold his possessions to fund missions overseas. When asked why, he said: *"I cannot take them with me, but I can send them ahead."* His surrender turned earthly wealth into eternal treasure.

Invitation – Living Generously

To overcome greed, we must practice detachment: using possessions without being possessed by them, and living with open hands before God.

Ask yourself:

- *Do I cling too tightly to money, status, or security?*

- *Am I willing to let go, trusting God as my true treasure?*

- *How can I practice generosity today in imitation of Christ's surrender?*

Closing Prayer

Father of Mercy, into Your hands I commend my spirit. Free me from greed and grasping, teach me to live with open hands, and let my wealth be found in love. May I surrender all I have and am to You, as Christ did upon the Cross. **Amen.**

PART II

Practicing Virtue

Introduction

The Cross does more than free us from sin; it strengthens us to grow in virtue. Every nail, every wound, every word of Christ on Calvary is an invitation to live differently — to embody faith, hope, charity, and the other virtues that make us sons and daughters of God.

Archbishop Sheen often taught that holiness is not a single heroic act, but a habit of daily fidelity. Virtue is the steady flame that burns in the soul, even in the darkness. These meditations will help us see how the grace of the Cross can shape our thoughts, our actions, and our character, until Christ Himself is formed within us.

- Reflection 1 – Practicing the Virtue of Fortitude

- Reflection 2 – Practicing the Virtue of Hope

- Reflection 3 – Practicing the Virtue of Prudence

- Reflection 4 – Practicing the Virtue of Faith

- Reflection 5 – Practicing the Virtue of Temperance

- Reflection 6 – Practicing the Virtue of Justice

- Reflection 7 – Practicing the Virtue of Charity

REFLECTION 1

Practicing the Virtue of Fortitude

The First Word: *"Father, forgive them, for they know not what they do."*

Reflection – Courage in the Face of Injustice

Fortitude is not the absence of fear but the strength to remain faithful in the face of suffering. On Calvary, Jesus demonstrated fortitude not by striking back at His enemies but by forgiving them. True courage is not retaliation, but endurance rooted in love.

To forgive in the midst of pain requires a heroism greater than violence. The Cross teaches us that fortitude is the power to face hatred without losing charity.

Sheen on Fortitude in the First Word

> *"The true courage of Christ was not in avoiding the Cross but in mounting it. Not in calling down fire upon His enemies, but in forgiving them. Fortitude is not the defiance of pain, but the endurance of it for love's sake."*

Archbishop Sheen saw fortitude as the foundation of the Christian life. Without it, every other virtue collapses under trial.

Illustration – A Martyr's Courage

St. Stephen, the first martyr, echoed the words of Christ: *"Lord, do not hold this sin against them."* (Acts 7:60) In his moment of death, Stephen revealed the fortitude of the Cross — courage not to curse his killers, but to bless them.

This same spirit is possible in our lives, in smaller sacrifices, when we respond to injustice with patience and love.

Invitation – Learning

Courage in Forgiveness

Fortitude is not only for martyrs. It is for parents enduring hardship, workers facing ridicule, the sick bearing pain, and every Christian asked to forgive. To practice fortitude is to stand firm at Calvary with Christ.

Ask yourself:

- *Do I meet trials with courage, or with resentment?*

- *Can I forgive those who wrong me, even when it costs me dearly?*

- *Am I willing to be strong not by striking back, but by enduring in love?*

Closing Prayer

Lord Jesus, You showed fortitude on the Cross by forgiving Your enemies in love. Grant me courage to face my trials, strength to endure my sufferings, and the grace to forgive as You forgave. Let me be strong not in anger, but in mercy. **Amen.**

REFLECTION 2

Practicing the Virtue of Hope

The Second Word: *"This day you will be with Me in paradise."*

Reflection – Hope in the Face of Death

Hope looks beyond the present suffering to the promise of eternal life. On Calvary, when the good thief turned to Jesus with trust, he received the assurance of heaven: *"This day you will be with Me in paradise."*

Hope is not wishful thinking but confident trust in God's mercy. Even in our last hour, His love is greater than our sins.

Sheen on Hope in the Second Word

> *"One thief died in despair, the other in hope. Despair fixed its eyes on sin; hope fixed its eyes on the Savior. Hope does not deny the past but trusts in mercy stronger than sin."*

Archbishop Sheen stressed that hope is always possible, no matter how dark the hour, because salvation rests not on our worthiness but on Christ's Cross.

Illustration – Conversion at the End

A man estranged from the Church for decades received the Sacraments on his deathbed. Whispering the prayer of the thief — *"Remember me, Lord"* — he died in peace. His story shows that hope is never too late, and that heaven is open to all who turn to Christ.

Invitation – Living Hope Daily

Hope is not only for the dying but for the living. It calls us to trust God's promises in our daily struggles — in sickness, in failure, in sin. To live with hope is to believe that every cross is the doorway to paradise.

Ask yourself:

- *Do I allow despair to cloud my view of God's mercy?*

- *Where do I need to place more trust in His promises?*

- *Am I living as one who believes in heaven?*

Closing Prayer

Lord Jesus, You gave hope to the thief on the Cross. Give me hope in every trial, trust in every failure, and confidence in Your mercy. Let my last breath echo his prayer: "Remember me, Lord, when You come into Your kingdom." **Amen.**

REFLECTION 3

Practicing the Virtue of Prudence

The Third Word: *"Behold your Mother."*

Reflection – The Wisdom of Love

Prudence is the virtue of choosing rightly, guided by truth and love. On Calvary, Jesus entrusted His Mother to John and John to His Mother. In this act, He revealed prudence at its highest — not self-preservation, but the wise care of souls.

Prudence sees beyond the moment. It considers God's will, the needs of others, and the eternal consequences of our choices.

Sheen on Prudence in the Third Word

> *"Prudence is not mere caution, but right reason in action. Our Lord, in His dying wisdom, provided for His Mother and His Church. He showed that prudence is love seeing far ahead, love preparing for the future."*

Archbishop Sheen explained that true prudence is never selfish calculation, but the wise ordering of all things toward God.

Illustration – A Saint's Wise Choice

St. Maximilian Kolbe, in Auschwitz, offered his life in place of a condemned prisoner. His prudence was not worldly strategy but supernatural wisdom: recognizing that to save another's life was to fulfill God's will.

His act, like Christ's word to Mary and John, shows prudence as love expressed in wise sacrifice.

Invitation – Choosing in the Light of the Cross

To practice prudence is to let the Cross guide our decisions. It means asking not, *"What is easiest?"* but *"What is truest, holiest, most loving?"*

Ask yourself:

- *Do I make choices based on comfort or on God's will?*

- *Am I seeking the eternal good of others, as Jesus did for His Mother?*

- *How can I let prudence guide me in small daily decisions?*

Closing Prayer

Lord Jesus, in Your wisdom You gave us Your Mother. Teach me prudence in my choices, that I may seek what is true, choose what is holy, and act always in love. May my decisions reflect the wisdom of Calvary. **Amen.**

REFLECTION 4

Practicing the Virtue of Faith

The Fourth Word: *"My God, My God, why have You forsaken Me?"*

Reflection – Trust in Darkness

Faith is not proven when everything is clear, but when God seems silent. On the Cross, Jesus cried out the words of Psalm 22 — the prayer of the suffering just man. Though He felt the weight of abandonment, He entrusted Himself still to the Father.

Faith does not remove the darkness; it holds firm within it. At Calvary, Christ shows that to believe in the Father amid silence is the highest act of trust.

Sheen on Faith in the Fourth Word

> *"The greatest act of faith is to trust when there is no sign, no consolation, no answer. Our Lord's cry was not despair, but faith — faith clinging to the Father when the Father seemed absent."*

Archbishop Sheen often said that true faith is forged in trial. Like Christ on the Cross, the believer says: *"I do not see, but I still believe."*

Illustration – The Dark Night of Faith

St. Teresa of Calcutta endured decades of spiritual dryness, often feeling abandoned by God. Yet she continued her mission with unwavering fidelity, loving the poorest of the poor. Her faith was not based on feelings, but on trust — the same faith Jesus lived on Calvary.

Invitation – Believing in the Silence

Faith calls us to trust when prayers seem unanswered, when trials press heavy, when God feels distant. To practice faith is to echo Jesus' cry, turning apparent absence into an offering of love.

Ask yourself:

- *Do I measure faith by feelings, or by fidelity?*

- *Am I willing to trust God even when He seems far away?*

- *How can I let my trials become acts of deeper faith?*

Closing Prayer

My God, when You seem far, teach me to believe. When I feel abandoned, let me cling to You in trust. May my faith be steady, not in consolations, but in Your Cross, where love endures even in silence. **Amen.**

REFLECTION 5

Practicing the Virtue of Temperance

The Fifth Word: *"I thirst."*

Reflection – Desire Ordered by Love

Temperance is the virtue that governs our desires, directing them toward what is truly good. On the Cross, Jesus spoke of thirst — not merely physical, but spiritual. He thirsted for souls, for love, for the fulfillment of the Father's will.

In Christ's cry, we learn that temperance is not the denial of desire, but its transformation. Our hearts find satisfaction only when their thirst is for God.

Sheen on Temperance in the Fifth Word

> *"When Our Lord said, 'I thirst,' He revealed the deepest longing of His Heart — for our love. Temperance is not the extinction of desire, but its sanctification. Our Lord's thirst teaches us to crave not the things of earth, but the things of heaven."*

Archbishop Sheen taught that Christ purifies our desires, lifting them from selfish satisfaction to self-giving love.

Illustration – A Saint's Thirst

St. Augustine, who once sought pleasure in the world, found peace only in God. He prayed: *"You have made us for Yourself, O Lord, and our hearts are restless until they rest in You."* His conversion is a witness to temperance — desires ordered by grace toward eternal love.

Invitation – Purifying My Desires

Temperance is lived when we discipline our appetites, moderating what is good and rejecting what enslaves us. Above all, it is lived when our deepest thirst is for God's love.

Ask yourself:

- *What desires in my life need to be purified?*

- *Do I thirst more for the world's pleasures or for God's will?*

- *How can I let Christ redirect my desires to what truly satisfies?*

Closing Prayer

O Jesus, who thirsted for souls upon the Cross, purify my desires. Teach me to hunger and thirst for righteousness, to crave Your love above all else, and to order my life toward You. Let my thirst be joined to Yours, until it is quenched in eternity. **Amen.**

REFLECTION 6

Practicing the Virtue of Justice

The Sixth Word: *"It is finished."*

Reflection – Giving What Is Due

Justice is the virtue of rendering to God and to others what is rightfully theirs. On Calvary, Jesus declared: *"It is finished."* In that moment, He fulfilled justice perfectly — giving to the Father complete obedience, and to humanity complete redemption.

Justice is not merely about fairness but about fidelity: giving God our worship, our neighbor our love, and fulfilling our duties with integrity.

Sheen on Justice in the Sixth Word

> *"Justice was satisfied on the Cross, not by a balance of scales, but by the gift of a life. Our Lord paid the debt of sin, rendering to the Father perfect love and to mankind perfect mercy."*

Archbishop Sheen explained that the Cross reveals justice not as cold law, but as love fulfilling every demand of truth.

Illustration – A Life Well Finished

St. Paul could say at the end of his life: *"I have fought the good fight, I have finished the race, I have kept the faith."* (2 Tim 4:7) His perseverance reflected Christ's justice — finishing the work entrusted to him, giving God and man what was due.

Invitation – Living Justice Daily

Justice is practiced when we fulfill our obligations: to God in prayer and worship, to others in honesty and charity, to ourselves in integrity. To live justly is to finish our tasks with faithfulness, however small.

Ask yourself:

- *Am I faithful in giving God His due through prayer and worship?*

- *Do I fulfill my duties toward others with honesty and charity?*

- *Am I living with the goal of finishing well, as Christ did?*

Closing Prayer

Lord Jesus, You finished the work of our redemption. Teach me to live justly: faithful to God, honest with others, true to my calling. Grant me perseverance to finish my race, and at the end, to hear You say: "It is finished." **Amen.**

REFLECTION 7

Practicing the Virtue of Charity

The Seventh Word: *"Father, into Your hands I commend My spirit."*

Reflection – Love Surrendered Completely

Charity is the greatest of the virtues, binding all the others together. On Calvary, Jesus' final word was one of surrender — giving Himself entirely into the Father's hands. In that act, His love was complete: for the Father, for humanity, for every soul He came to redeem.

Charity is not sentiment but self-giving. It is the willingness to place all we are and all we have into God's hands.

Sheen on Charity in the Seventh Word

> *"Charity is the soul of all virtue. Faith and hope will pass away, but charity will endure forever. On the Cross, charity reached its fullness as Our Lord surrendered His spirit to the Father for love of us."*

Archbishop Sheen explained that the Cross is charity incarnate — love giving itself without limit, even unto death.

Illustration – A Saint's Final Offering

St. Thérèse of Lisieux, in her last moments, whispered: *"My God, I love You."* Her little way culminated in this final act of charity, surrendering her life into the hands of God with childlike trust.

Her death, like Christ's final word, shows that charity is the perfection of Christian life: to die in love, as we have lived in love.

Invitation – Living Charity as Surrender

To practice charity is to love God above all and neighbor as oneself. It means surrendering our will, our possessions, our time, our hearts into God's hands, confident that love is never lost in Him.

Ask yourself:

- *Am I willing to surrender everything into God's hands in love?*

- *How can I practice charity not only in words, but in daily sacrifices?*

- *Do I see charity as the crown of all virtues, the goal of my life?*

Closing Prayer

Father of Love, into Your hands I commend my spirit. Teach me to live in charity, to surrender my life as an offering of love, and to give myself without reserve, as Christ did upon the Cross. May charity crown my days, and be my final word at life's end. **Amen.**

PART III

Living the Beatitudes

Introduction

When Jesus first proclaimed the Beatitudes on the Mount, He described the way of life that leads to blessedness. On Calvary, He lived them all. Poverty of spirit, mercy, purity of heart, meekness, and even persecution — each found its fulfillment in the Crucified.

The Beatitudes are not soft ideals but heroic virtues, shining most brightly at the Cross. To live them is to embrace the paradox of Christian life: to find joy in sacrifice, strength in meekness, and eternal reward in seeming loss. These reflections invite us to walk with Christ from the Mount of the Beatitudes to the Hill of Calvary, and to let His blessings shape our lives.

- Reflection 1 – Blessed are the meek, for they shall inherit the earth

- Reflection 2 – Blessed are the merciful, for they shall obtain mercy

- Reflection 3 – Blessed are the pure in heart, for they shall see God

- Reflection 4 – Blessed are the poor in spirit, for theirs is the kingdom of heaven

- Reflection 5 – Blessed are those who hunger and thirst for justice, for they shall be satisfied

- Reflection 6 – Blessed are the peacemakers, for they shall be called children of God

- Reflection 7 – Blessed are those who mourn, for they shall be comforted

- Reflection 8 – Blessed are those who are persecuted for righteousness' sake, for theirs is the kingdom of heaven

REFLECTION 1

Living the Beatitude:
Blessed are the meek,
for they shall inherit the earth.

The First Word: *"Father, forgive them, for they know not what they do."*

Reflection – Meekness as Strength Under Control

Meekness is not weakness. It is the strength of the soul under discipline, refusing to answer violence with violence. On Calvary, Jesus revealed meekness in perfection: in the midst of brutality and injustice, He responded not with wrath but with forgiveness.

Meekness disarms anger and calms hatred. It inherits the earth not by conquest but by mercy.

Sheen on Meekness in the First Word

> *"The world believes the strong man is the one who strikes back. Christ taught that the meek man is the one who can dominate himself. By forgiving, He conquered anger; by being silent, He conquered pride."*

Archbishop Sheen explained that meekness does not destroy justice but fulfills it through mercy.

Illustration – The Strength of Meekness

Mahatma Gandhi once remarked that the Sermon on the Mount was the greatest sermon on nonviolence. Yet it is on Calvary, in Jesus' meek forgiveness, that its truth is revealed most fully. Christian meekness is not passive but active love, turning enemies into brothers.

Invitation – Practicing Meekness in My Life

Meekness is lived in our homes, our workplaces, and our parishes when we choose patience over harshness, forgiveness over retaliation, gentleness over cruelty.

Ask yourself:

- *Do I lash out when wronged, or do I seek meekness in response?*

- *Am I willing to let go of vengeance for the sake of peace?*

- *How can I imitate Christ's meekness in daily conflicts?*

Closing Prayer

Lord Jesus, meek and humble of heart, You forgave those who crucified You. Teach me to be meek, to master my anger, and to conquer hatred with love. Grant that I may inherit the peace of Your kingdom, not by force, but by mercy. **Amen.**

REFLECTION 2

Living the Beatitude:
Blessed are the merciful,
for they shall obtain mercy.

The Second Word: *"This day you will be with Me in Paradise."*

Reflection – Mercy in the Face of Sin

Mercy is love bending down to lift misery. On Calvary, the good thief confessed his guilt and asked only to be remembered. Jesus answered with mercy far greater than he hoped: *"This day you will be with Me in Paradise."*

Mercy does not excuse sin, but heals it. It looks at misery with compassion, not scorn, and opens heaven where there was only despair.

Sheen on Mercy in the Second Word

> *"The thief had nothing to recommend him — no good works, no defense, no future. But he had one thing: faith in mercy. And mercy did not disappoint. Mercy is love answering sin with forgiveness."*

Archbishop Sheen stressed that mercy is not weakness but the very strength of God's love poured out upon the unworthy.

Illustration – Mercy at the Last Hour

A priest once told of being called to the bedside of a hardened sinner. With tears, the man whispered, *"Father, forgive me."* He died shortly after receiving absolution. Like the good thief, he entered eternity clinging to mercy alone.

Invitation – Practicing Mercy Daily

Mercy is not only for God to give, but for us to share. To practice mercy is to forgive others, to comfort the sorrowful, to bear wrongs patiently, and to remember that as we give, so we shall receive.

Ask yourself:

- *Do I withhold mercy from those who wrong me?*

- *Am I quick to judge, or quick to forgive?*

- *How can I show mercy in concrete ways to those around me?*

Closing Prayer

Lord Jesus, You showed mercy to the thief on the Cross. Show mercy also to me in my weakness. Help me to forgive as I have been forgiven, to love as I have been loved, and to obtain mercy by practicing mercy. **Amen.**

REFLECTION 3

Living the Beatitude:
Blessed are the pure in heart,
for they shall see God.

The Third Word: *"Behold your Mother."*

Reflection – Purity as Undivided Love

Purity of heart is not merely freedom from lust but freedom from all duplicity, all self-seeking. At Calvary, Jesus gave His Mother to John, and John to His Mother — a bond of love undefiled, a new family born from the Cross.

Purity means to see others as God sees them — as gifts, not objects; as persons, not possessions. To be pure in heart is to live with undivided love.

Sheen on Purity in the Third Word

> *"Purity is not the absence of passion but the re-direction of it. The impure heart sees flesh; the pure heart sees souls. On the Cross, Our Lord lifted love to its highest by giving us His Mother."*

Archbishop Sheen emphasized that purity of heart enables us to see God not only in heaven, but here on earth, in His image reflected in others.

Illustration – A Life of Pure Devotion

St. Maria Goretti, a young martyr for chastity, forgave her attacker as she lay dying. Her heart, pure and undivided, saw God even in her moment of trial. Her life remains a testament to the Beatitude of purity.

Invitation – Seeking Purity of Heart

Purity of heart demands vigilance, prayer, and sacrifice. But it is also a gift — the grace to see with clear eyes, to love without selfishness, and to live with a heart set on God.

Ask yourself:

- *Do I seek to see others with pure eyes and love them as God's children?*

- *Are there attachments or sins clouding my heart's vision?*

- *Am I asking daily for the grace to live with a clean heart?*

Closing Prayer

Lord Jesus, You gave us Your Mother from the Cross. Through her intercession, create in me a clean heart. Help me to see You in others, to love without selfishness, and to live with a heart undivided.
Amen.

REFLECTION 4

Living the Beatitude:
Blessed are the poor in spirit,
for theirs is the kingdom
of heaven.

The Fourth Word: *"My God, My God, why have You forsaken Me?"*

Reflection – Poverty of Spirit as Dependence on God

To be poor in spirit is to recognize our utter need for God. On Calvary, Jesus entered into the deepest poverty: stripped of comfort, abandoned by friends, and even feeling the silence of the Father. Yet in this poverty, He clung to faith, entrusting Himself completely to God.

Poverty of spirit is not misery, but freedom — freedom from self-reliance, freedom to trust God in everything.

Sheen on Poverty of Spirit in the Fourth Word

> *"The cry of abandonment was not despair, but the prayer of the poor in spirit. Christ, bereft of every comfort, clung still to the Father. The poor in spirit are those who, having nothing, possess everything in God."*

Archbishop Sheen explained that the kingdom belongs to the poor in spirit because they rely entirely on the King.

Illustration – Faith in the Midst of Loss

A widow who lost her husband and children in war said, *"I have nothing left — but I still have God."* Her poverty of spirit did not destroy her but made her a living witness of faith in God's sufficiency.

Invitation – Choosing Poverty of Spirit

To live this Beatitude is to hold earthly goods lightly and to seek our true security in God alone. It is to say with Christ, even in desolation: *"My God."*

Ask yourself:

- *Do I cling to possessions, achievements, or control for security?*

- *Am I willing to let God be enough, even when everything else fails?*

- *How can I practice poverty of spirit in daily life?*

Closing Prayer

My God, when I feel abandoned, teach me to trust You. Grant me the poverty of spirit that clings to You alone. May I find my treasure not in possessions, but in Your kingdom. **Amen.**

REFLECTION 5

Living the Beatitude:
Blessed are those who hunger
and thirst for justice,
for they shall be satisfied.

The Fifth Word: *"I thirst."*

Reflection – Holy Desire that Satisfies

Jesus' cry of thirst was not only for water but for righteousness, for souls, for the fulfillment of the Father's will. This Beatitude calls us to cultivate holy desires, to thirst not for fleeting pleasures but for justice, truth, and holiness.

Those who hunger and thirst for justice are never left empty — for their desire aligns with God's own Heart.

Sheen on Holy Desire in the Fifth Word

> *"The world is full of thirsts which never satisfy — the thirst for pleasure, for power, for wealth. But only one thirst satisfies: the thirst for justice, which is the thirst for God Himself."*

Archbishop Sheen taught that to hunger for justice is to direct our desires to their highest fulfillment — in Christ, who alone satisfies.

Illustration – A Saint's Burning Thirst

St. Catherine of Siena once prayed: *"My Lord, I hunger for souls."* Her holy thirst drove her to serve the poor, reform the Church, and counsel popes. Her life was a testimony that to thirst for God's justice is to be filled with His strength.

Invitation – Purifying My Desires

To live this Beatitude is to examine what we hunger for. Earthly desires leave us empty, but the thirst for holiness, truth, and love fills us with God.

Ask yourself:

- *What do I thirst for most deeply?*

- *Are my desires ordered toward God or toward myself?*

- *How can I redirect my hunger to seek holiness above all?*

Closing Prayer

O Jesus, who thirsted for souls upon the Cross, give me a thirst for holiness. Satisfy my hunger with Your justice, and fill me with the joy that comes only from You. **Amen.**

REFLECTION 6

Living the Beatitude: Blessed are the peacemakers, for they shall be called children of God.

The Sixth Word: *"It is finished."*

Reflection – Peace Through Completion

Peace is not the absence of conflict but the presence of wholeness. On Calvary, Jesus declared: *"It is finished."* He completed the work of redemption, reconciling heaven and earth. In that moment, true peace was made: the peace of the Cross.

Peacemakers are those who bring reconciliation — not by avoiding sacrifice, but by finishing the work of love, even when it costs.

Sheen on Peacemaking in the Sixth Word

> *"Peace is the tranquility of order. On the Cross, Christ put all things in order by doing the Father's will to the end. The greatest peacemakers are those who bring others into harmony with God."*

Archbishop Sheen taught that peace cannot be built on compromise with sin, but only on truth lived to completion.

Illustration – A Bridge of Peace

St. Francis of Assisi once went unarmed into the camp of the Muslim sultan during the Crusades, risking death to proclaim Christ. Though they disagreed, the sultan honored him as a man of peace. Francis' courage showed that peacemaking is not cowardice but the fruit of fidelity.

Invitation – Becoming a Peacemaker

To live this Beatitude is to finish the tasks of love, to build bridges of reconciliation, and to bear the cost of peace.

Ask yourself:

- *Do I avoid conflict at the expense of truth?*

- *Am I willing to pay the price of bringing peace where there is division?*

- *How can I finish the work of love in my family, parish, or community?*

Closing Prayer

Lord Jesus, You finished the work of redemption and brought peace to the world. Make me a peacemaker, willing to bear the cost of reconciliation. Let me be called a child of God by sowing peace in Your name. **Amen.**

REFLECTION 7

Living the Beatitude:
Blessed are those who mourn,
for they shall be comforted.

The Seventh Word: *"Father, into Your hands I commend My spirit."*

Reflection – Mourning Transformed by Trust

Mourning is the cry of the heart over loss, sin, and suffering. On Calvary, Jesus entered into the deepest sorrow as He surrendered His life into the Father's hands. Yet even in that final breath, sorrow was not despair but trust.

The Beatitude promises comfort to those who mourn because God Himself enters into their grief, turning tears into seeds of hope.

Sheen on Mourning in the Seventh Word

> *"Sorrow without faith leads to despair; sorrow with faith leads to comfort. Christ sanctified mourning by His own death, showing that tears can be pearls when placed in the hands of the Father."*

Archbishop Sheen explained that Christian mourning is not hopelessness, but the path to consolation in God.

Illustration – Tears that Became Prayer

A mother wept for years over her son who had abandoned the faith. At last, he returned to the sacraments before dying. Her mourning was turned to consolation, echoing the words of Scripture: *"Those who sow in tears shall reap rejoicing."* (Ps. 126:5)

Invitation – Mourning with Hope

To live this Beatitude is to bring our griefs, our sins, and our losses into God's hands. He alone can transform mourning into comfort.

Ask yourself:

- *Do I allow sorrow to lead me to God, or do I let it turn to despair?*

- *What grief do I need to place into the Father's hands?*

- *Can I trust that He will bring comfort even from my tears?*

Closing Prayer

Father of Consolation, into Your hands I commend my spirit. Take my sorrows and transform them, my tears and sanctify them, my mourning and comfort it with Your love. **Amen.**

REFLECTION 8

Living the Beatitude: Blessed are those who are persecuted for righteousness' sake, for theirs is the kingdom of heaven.

"And bowing His head, He gave up His spirit."

Reflection – Persecution Embraced in Love

Persecution comes when the world resists truth. On Calvary, Jesus was persecuted not for wrongdoing, but for righteousness — for being the Truth itself. His last breath sanctified every sacrifice made by those who suffer for His name.

The Beatitude promises that persecution is not defeat, but a share in Christ's victory. The kingdom belongs to those who, like Him, remain faithful unto death.

Sheen on Persecution in the Final Word

> *"The world may tolerate a watered-down gospel, but it will always crucify righteousness. Our Lord's last breath was His triumph over persecution, for it proved that death could not conquer truth."*

Archbishop Sheen often reminded Christians that fidelity will draw opposition, but the Cross transforms suffering into glory.

Illustration – Witness in Martyrdom

The early martyrs of Rome faced brutal deaths for refusing to deny Christ. As they perished, they sang hymns of joy. Their persecutors thought them defeated, but the blood of the martyrs became the seed of the Church.

Invitation – Faithful in Trial

To live this Beatitude is to accept that following Christ will bring opposition, yet to remain steadfast with love.

Ask yourself:

- *Am I willing to suffer ridicule or rejection for my faith?*

- *Do I compromise truth to avoid persecution?*

- *How can I stand firm in righteousness with love, not bitterness?*

Closing Prayer

Lord Jesus, You were persecuted unto death, Yet you triumphed in love. Strengthen me when I face opposition, make me steadfast in righteousness, and grant me courage to share in Your Cross, that I too may inherit the kingdom of heaven. **Amen.**

EPILOGUE

The Cross and the
Christian Way of Life

The Cross does not leave us where it finds us. It frees us from the slavery of sin, strengthens us to practice virtue, and blesses us with the joy of the Beatitudes. Every step we take in overcoming anger, envy, lust, pride, gluttony, sloth, or greed; every effort to live faith, hope, charity, prudence, justice, temperance, and fortitude; every attempt to embody the spirit of the Beatitudes — all of it is a share in the victory of Calvary.

Archbishop Fulton Sheen often reminded us that holiness is not an idea but a way of life. The Cross is not only a mystery to be adored, it is a pattern to be lived. To overcome sin, to grow in virtue, to live the Beatitudes — this is to let the Crucified live in us.

May these reflections lead you not only to the foot of the Cross, but into a life shaped by it. And may you discover, as countless saints before you, that the Cross embraced with love is the surest path to joy, peace, and eternal glory.

Closing Word

As you bring this retreat journey to a close, remember that the end is not an ending, but a beginning. The gaze upon the Holy Face, the companionship of Mary, the embrace of the Cross, and the light of the Eucharist are not chapters to be finished, but mysteries to be lived.

Do not worry if your steps have been uneven or your reading imperfect. God works with what we offer, however small. A single glance of love, a brief moment of prayer, a whispered act of reparation — these, too, have eternal weight.

Carry forward what you have received. Let these meditations become seeds of silence, patience, courage, and charity in your daily life. The world is longing for souls who reflect the light of Christ.

"The only tragedy in life is not to be a saint."

— Archbishop Fulton J. Sheen

May this book be for you not only a retreat, but a lifelong companion in your mission of reparation and love.

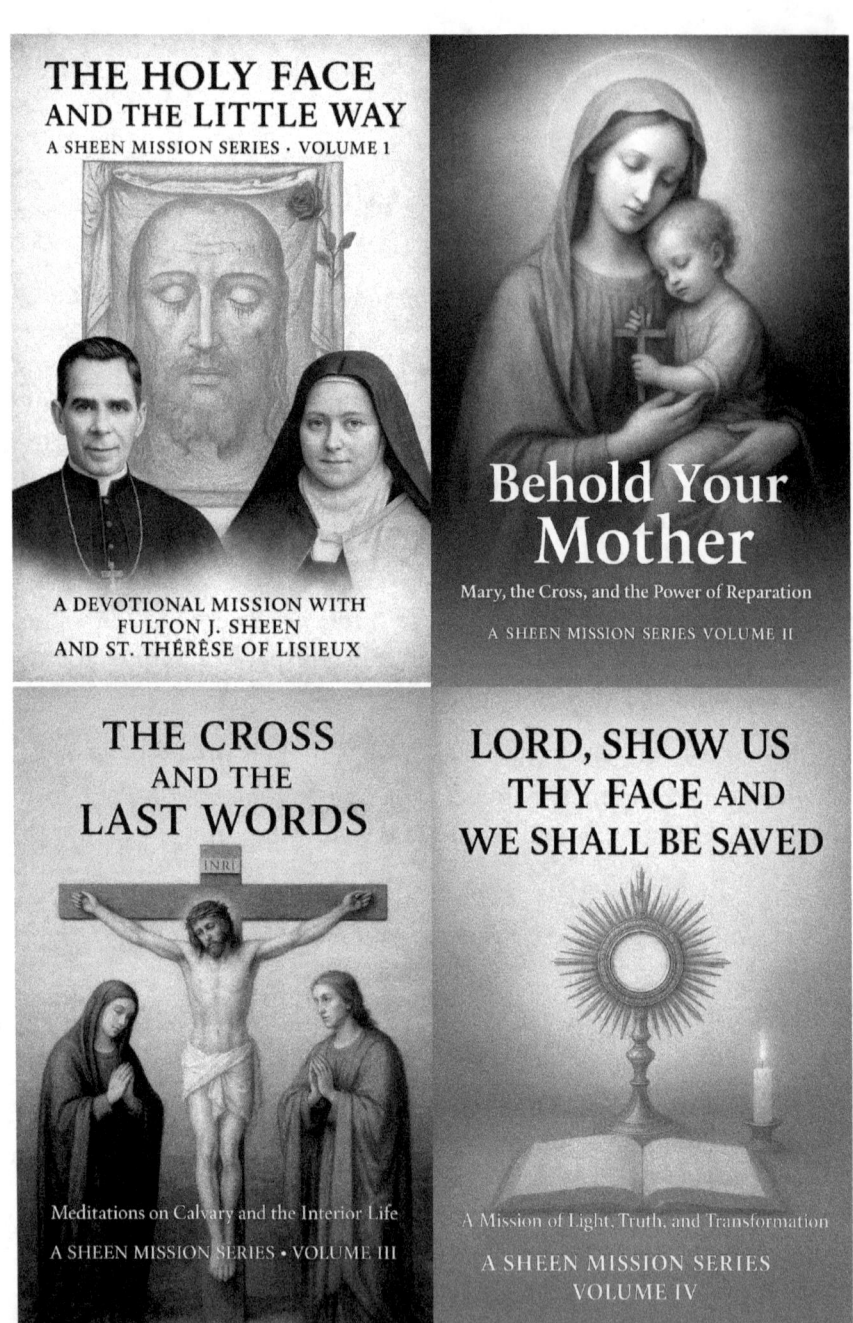

THE HOLY FACE AND THE LITTLE WAY
A SHEEN MISSION SERIES · VOLUME 1

A DEVOTIONAL MISSION WITH
FULTON J. SHEEN
AND ST. THÉRÈSE OF LISIEUX

Behold Your Mother
Mary, the Cross, and the Power of Reparation
A SHEEN MISSION SERIES VOLUME II

THE CROSS AND THE LAST WORDS
Meditations on Calvary and the Interior Life
A SHEEN MISSION SERIES · VOLUME III

LORD, SHOW US THY FACE AND WE SHALL BE SAVED
A Mission of Light, Truth, and Transformation
A SHEEN MISSION SERIES
VOLUME IV

Praying This Book as a Retreat

This book is more than a collection of meditations — it is a companion for the soul's pilgrimage. Archbishop Fulton J. Sheen often urged the faithful to make a daily Holy Hour, and St. Thérèse of Lisieux showed us that every small act of love can become an offering of reparation. Together, they teach us that prayer is not escape but encounter — an entering into the silence where the Face of Christ is revealed.

The following retreat paths are offered as gentle rhythms for prayer. They are not strict programs, but invitations to slow down and let grace order your days.

- **Seven Days** – for a parish mission or personal retreat.

- **Twenty-Eight Days** – for a month-long journey, an Advent or seasonal renewal.

- **Forty Days (or 46 for Lent)** – for a pilgrimage from the Holy Face to the Beatitudes.

Each schedule now encompasses five movements of the Christian life — the Holy Face of Jesus, the Blessed Mother Mary, the Cross, the Eucharist, and the interior life, which involves overcoming sin, practicing virtue, and living the beatitudes. Use them during Adoration, in group settings, or within your own quiet prayer.

"Let Your Face shine upon us, Lord, and we shall be saved."

— Psalm 80:3

INTRODUCTION

A Retreat in Print

The five parts of this book trace a spiritual arc of conversion and communion:

1. **The Holy Face and the Little Way** – encountering Christ in hiddenness and love.

2. **Behold Your Mother** – standing with Mary at the Cross.

3. **The Cross and the Last Words** – entering the mystery of Calvary with Sheen.

4. **Lord, Show Us Thy Face and We Shall Be Saved** – living the Eucharistic mission of Christ in the world.

5. **Overcoming Sin, Practicing Virtue, and Living the Beatitudes** – the interior renewal that makes mission fruitful.

You may follow these parts consecutively or dwell on one theme at a time. Whether prayed in solitude, during Adoration, or within a community, the rhythm is the same: contemplation leading to imitation, silence leading to mission.

> *"Holiness begins at the altar and ends in the heart."*
>
> **— Archbishop Fulton J. Sheen**

You may read these parts in sequence as a sustained journey, or pause and dwell with one theme at a time.

For Daily Prayer

Archbishop Sheen often urged the faithful to make a **daily Holy Hour** before the Blessed Sacrament. This book is designed to support that practice. You might:

- Read one chapter slowly during your Holy Hour.

- Linger over the Scripture passages and allow silence to follow.

- Conclude with one of the prayers from this book.

Even if you cannot make a full Holy Hour, these meditations can be prayed in shorter moments throughout the day.

For Retreats

This collection lends itself well to parish missions, small-group retreats, or personal days of recollection. Each part can be used as a **retreat theme**—whether for one day, a triduum, or a full week of prayer.

A Word of Encouragement

Read slowly. Pray deeply. Let these pages lead you from contemplation to imitation, from silence before the Holy Face to mission in the world. As Archbishop Sheen taught, *"The greatest love story of all time is contained in a tiny white Host."* May this book help you to discover, day by day, that love story anew.

Retreat Schedules

SEVEN-DAY RETREAT

This plan offers a week of prayer, ideal for a parish mission, Holy Week preparation, or a personal retreat. Each day focuses on one pillar of the Christian journey: the Holy Face, Mary, the Cross, and the Eucharist.

Day	Focus	Readings / Meditations	Suggested Closing Prayer
1	The Holy Face	Part I – Introduction + Meditations 1–2	Litany of the Holy Face
2	Mary	Part II – Meditations 1–2	Hail Mary / Marian prayer
3	The Cross	Part III – Meditations 3–4	Prayer before the Crucifix
4	The Cross	Part III – Meditations 5–6	Litany of Reparation
5	Eucharist & Mission	Part IV – Meditations 1–5	Act of Consecration
6	Virtue & Interior Renewal	Part V – Reflections on Sin and Virtue 1–3	Act of Contrition / Prayer for Grace
7	The Beatitudes	Part V – Reflections on the Beatitudes	Benediction Hymn or Prayer of Mission

"The greatest love story of all time is contained in a tiny white Host."

— Fulton J. Sheen

TWENTY-EIGHT-DAY RETREAT

This schedule unfolds over four weeks, making space each day to reflect deeply on one or two meditations. It is well-suited for a month of recollection, the season of Advent, or a structured daily prayer rhythm.

Week	Focus	Daily Rhythm	Sunday Option
1	The Holy Face (Part I)	1–2 meditations per day	Review + Holy Face prayers
2	Mary at the Cross (Part II)	1–2 meditations per day	Rosary of the Seven Sorrows
3	The Cross and the Last Words (Part III)	2 -3 meditations per day	Stations of the Cross
4	Eucharist & Mission (Part IV) + Virtue and Beatitudes (Part V)	1 meditation from each section per day	Eucharistic adoration and Examination of Virtue

"Do not pass a day without making some sacrifice for the sake of souls."

— St. Thérèse of Lisieux

FORTY-DAY (LENTEN) JOURNEY

This extended plan follows the arc of Lent, leading the soul step by step from the Holy Face, through Mary and the Cross, to the Eucharistic mission of Christ. Perfect for the forty days of Lent (or forty-six including Sundays).

Days	Focus	Meditations / Themes	Notes
1–8	The Holy Face (Part I)	1 -2 meditations per day	Fridays: Litany of the Holy Face
9–16	Behold Your Mother (Part II)	1 -2 meditations per day	Saturdays: Marian devotions
17–28	The Cross (Part III)	2 -3 meditations per day	Fridays: Stations of the Cross
29–35	Eucharist & Mission (Part IV)	1 -2 meditations per day	Sundays: Eucharistic Adoration
36–40 (or 46)	Sin, Virtue & the Beatitudes (Part V)	2 -3 meditations per day	Final week: Daily Examen and Prayer for Renewal

"If you wish to know the love of Christ, kneel before His Cross."

— **Fulton J. Sheen**

About the Author

ALLAN SMITH is a Catholic evangelist, radio host, and spiritual director who has spent over a decade proclaiming the wisdom of Archbishop Fulton J. Sheen to audiences around the world. As the founder of Bishop Sheen Today, he has edited and published dozens of classic Sheen titles, including 'The Cries of Jesus from the Cross' and 'Lord, Teach Us to Pray'.

A passionate promoter of Eucharistic Reparation and devotion to the Holy Face of Jesus, Allan regularly speaks at parish missions, leads retreats, and hosts weekly radio broadcasts across Canada, the United States, Ireland, Australia and the Philippines. His work has helped reintroduce Sheen's powerful spiritual legacy to a new generation.

He lives in Canada with his family and continues his mission of calling souls to deeper intimacy with Christ through the example of saints like St. Thérèse of Lisieux and the timeless teachings of Archbishop Fulton J. Sheen.

To learn more or to access free devotional resources, visit our two websites at:

www.bishopsheentoday.com

www.holyfacemiracle.com

About the Sheen Mission Series

The Sheen Mission Series is a four-volume spiritual journey inspired by Archbishop Fulton J. Sheen. Each book is designed as a devotional companion — guiding the faithful in prayer, reparation, and renewal through the Holy Face of Jesus, the Cross, the Eucharist, and the maternal love of Our Blessed Mother.

The series can be read in any order, yet together it forms a complete mission of grace:

- **Volume I –** *The Holy Face and the Little Way*

- Walk with St. Thérèse of Lisieux in her Little Way of love, united to the devotion of the Holy Face of Jesus.

- **Volume II –** *Behold Your Mother*

- Enter into Mary's tender care at the foot of the Cross and discover the strength of her Seven Sorrows.

- **Volume III –** *The Cross and the Last Words*

- Pray with Archbishop Sheen at Calvary as he opens the treasures of the Seven Last Words of Christ.

- **Volume IV –** *Lord, Show Us Thy Face and We Shall Be Saved*

A mission of light and transformation, centred on the Eucharist and the saving power of Christ's Face.

The Sheen Mission Series invites you to walk with Archbishop Fulton J. Sheen in prayer, reparation, and renewal — a journey of the Holy Face, the Cross, the Eucharist, and Our Blessed Mother.

A Personal Invitation

Over the years, I have had the privilege of helping souls draw closer to Christ through prayer, silence, and the beautiful wisdom of Archbishop Fulton J. Sheen.

If this devotional has nourished your heart, you may also find these works helpful in your journey of faith:

Advent and Christmas with Archbishop Fulton J. Sheen
- A Devotional Journey of Waiting, Welcoming, and Living the Mystery

Daily readings and gentle reflections to guide the heart from hope to joy — from the quiet longing of Advent to the radiant wonder of Christmas.

Priest, Prophet & King
- Meditations on Identity, Mission, and the Call to Holiness

Reflections on what it means to truly belong to Christ — in our families, vocations, and daily life.

May every book you read be an open door to the heart of Christ.

May these works draw you deeper into prayer, trust, peace, and surrender.

To learn more or to stay connected:
www.bishopsheentoday.com

.

www.ingramcontent.com/pod-product-compliance
Lightning Source LLC
Chambersburg PA
CBHW071709120626
46550CB00001B/166

9 781997 931003